asianappetizers

starters and finger foods for every occasion

by Vicki Liley

PERIPLUS EDITIONS
Singapore • Hong Kong • Indonesia

Contents

All About Asian Appetizers

Appetizers are the heart of every party or get-together and are the enticing beginning to an elegant dinner. Light, tempting and full of flavor, they are traditionally served with drinks. But you don't need to have a party to enjoy delicious bites of food. Appetizers are ideal for brunch nibbles, mid-day snacks and light lunches, and they can be packed into a picnic basket and served at an impromptu barbecue or a small gathering of friends or family. Tempting morsels of food are welcome whatever the occasion or time of day and will make any event more enjoyable and memorable.

Bite-sized bundles of food are a hallmark of Asian cuisine. What would Asian food be without their crispy spring rolls or the silken wontons? In China, small dumplings and rolls have been served with tea since the Sung Dynasty in the tenth century.

If you have a passion for spices and the contrasting textures, colors, smells and cooking techniques of Asia, you will be delighted with offerings in this book. Add to that the ease of working with pre-made wonton skins or spring roll wrappers, and the Western convenience of unleavened breads and ready-made puff and filo pastries, and you have a great way of saving time, money and kitchen fuss. Perhaps the greatest bonus of embracing these no-fuss ways of wrapping, rolling and bundling small bites of food is that you'll have a convenient and fun means of introducing spicy Asian flavors and unusual ingredients to your friends and family—even the kids.

Use this book as a starting point for your own culinary inventions. Be brave and experiment with different foods and food combinations. You can even extend the fun by making appetizers an interactive event! Involve your guests or family in wrapping the dumplings or rolls by arranging the ingredients in serving dishes and letting everyone assemble their own. Accompany your offerings with a range of tasty dipping sauces, and sit back and reap the satisfaction of having everyone rave about the food.

What's on Your Appetizer Menu?

If you are planning a party, or deciding on an appetizer to start off a special meal, remember that people generally like to eat hot and filling foods in the winter, but may prefer light, cold appetizers in the summer months. For parties, it's good to calculate the number of appetizers by allotting four to six bite-sized servings per person for each hour you anticipate the gathering or occasion will last. You can offer fewer servings for larger finger foods, and it's a good idea to have back-up foods for unexpectedly large appetites.

Remember that simple appetizers that make the most of what's in season are always a wise choice. Four to five different appetizers, made in multiples and displayed in lines on large platters, will look magnificent and will certainly be within your budget. Plan a contrast of textures, such as soft and crisp or smooth and rough, and include a variety of colors and flavors. A combination of Spiced Bar Nuts, Chicken Yakitori Skewers, Baked Pork Roll-ups and Thai Beef Salad Wraps are delicious selections that provide great textures, flavors and colors.

Containing a wonderful variety of recipes, this book will give you the confidence to host large or small parties, and even cater for that special guest or friend. I show you how to make quick-and-easy finger foods, delectable dipping sauces and elegant appetizers that are rolled or wrapped, or prepared and then served on skewers. From the recipes to the preparation tips, you'll discover everything you need to guarantee a wonderful and successful party.

Happy cooking!

Essential Ingredients

Bird's-eye chilies are small and blazingly hot, with a clear fiery taste. Use in small quantities and remove the seeds if you wish to reduce the burn!.

Black dried Chinese mushrooms are strongly flavored, so use sparingly. Soak in hot water for 15–20 minutes to reconstitute. Discard the hard stems and squeeze the excess water from the caps before use.

Bonito flakes are dried sandy brown flakes of smoked bonito fish that are used to make dashi, which is the basic Japanese soup stock. The taste is almost akin to a fine smoked ham or dried beef.

Cellophane noodles are thin, translucent dried noodles made from mung beans. Also known as bean thread noodles. Cellophane noodles are delicious deep-fried and used in fillings for a crisp texture or as a crunchy bed for stir-fries. Or, soften them in hot water and use in soups, stir-fries, and fillings. Use rice stick vermicelli or angel hair pasta if unavailable.

Chickpea flour, also known as besan flour or gram flour, is made from dried chickpeas that are ground to a fine yellow flour rich in protein and dietary fiber. The flour has a slightly nutty flavor and is often used as an ingredient in batters, pastries and doughs.

Chinese barbecued pork, also known as char siew, is marinated in sweet soy before it is roasted. Sold sliced or whole in Chinese delis, it requires no further cooking. Store in the refrigerator for up to 2 days. Other types of sweet barbecued pork may be substituted.

Chili oil is an extremely hot oil, used in small quantities to flavor sauces. Made by frying chilies in either sesame or vegetable oil.

Chinese black vinegar is made from rice, wheat, and millet or sorghum. The best black vinegars are well-aged and have a complex, smoky flavor similar to balsamic, which may be substituted. Chinese cooks add black vinegar to sauces, dips and when braising meats.

Chili peppers come in many shapes, sizes and colors. Fresh green and red **Asian finger-length chilies** (also known as Thai chilies) are moderately hot and are available fresh in most supermarkets now.

Chinese rice wine, also known as Shaoxing wine. is a Chinese rice wine that is aged for at least 10 years. Can be substituted with dry sherry or sake. Available from Asian food stores.

Chinese roast duck is sold in Chinese takeaway restaurants, where it can often be seen hanging in the front window. May be purchased whole or by weight, chopped or in pieces.

Delicious on its own or use in fillings or salads. Store in the refrigerator for up to 2 days. Use barbecued chicken if unavailable.

Chinese roast pork is usually baked pork belly that has a crisp crackling crust. Often seen hanging in the window of Chinatown restaurants, it is sold by weight, sliced or whole. Substitute Chinese barbecued pork or roast pork slices from a regular deli.

Coriander leaves are also known as cilantro or Chinese parsley. Available fresh, the roots, stems and leaves are all used in cooking. They are strongly flavored, so use sparingly. Available in most supermarkets—but if you cannot find, use regular parsley with a few fresh basil leaves added.

Curry powder is a commercial spice blend that generally includes cumin, coriander, turmeric, ginger, cinnamon and cloves. Different combinations vary in color and flavor and are used for different types of curries—meat, fish or chicken. Use an all-purpose blend if a specific curry powder is not available. Store in an airtight container in the refrigerator.

Dried shrimp is a popular Asian ingredient used in sauces and sambals. These tiny, orange-colored sun-dried prawns keep for several months and should be soaked in water for 5 minutes to soften slightly before use. Look for dried shrimp that are pink and plump and avoid any grayish ones. Better quality ones are bright orange in color and fully shelled.

Filo pastry (also spelled phyllo) is a paper-thin dough made from flour and water, available frozen in supermarkets. Thaw in the refrigerator. Keep this dough covered with a damp cloth while working with it, as it dries out quickly.

Fish sauce is a pungent salty sauce extracted from fermented fish. It's used to enhance the flavor of dishes. Flavor and saltiness differ with different brands. Fish sauce from Thailand, called *nam pla*, is commonly available in most supermarkets today. Don't be put off by the strong fishy smell; there is really no substitute.

Fried noodles (flour sticks) are crispy fried noodles sold in packages in Asian food stores and commonly used as a garnish for Chinese dishes. If unavailable, simply deep-fry fresh egg noodles in hot oil until crisp.

Fried tofu pouches (aburaage) are thin squares of tofu that have been deep-fried so they are crisp on the outside but soft inside. They are sold in packets in the refrigerated sections of Asian food stores, and are used as pouches for fillings.

Garam masala is an Indian blend of powdered spices, usually including salt, cinnamon, cardamom, cloves, fennel and black pepper. Pre-blended garam masala can be bought from any store specializing in spices. Store in an airtight jar away from heat or sunlight. A bit of curry powder or ground fennel and cardamom mixed with salt may be used as a substitute.

Hoisin sauce is a sweet, thick, Chinese barbecue sauce made from soybeans, vinegar, sugar, chili and seasonings. Sold in cans and in bottles. Keeps well if refrigerated once opened.

Hot bean paste is a thick, red paste made from rice powder, fermented soybeans, red chili powder and salt, with small amounts of sugar or honey sometimes added. It forms the base for stews and marinades and is also used as a dressing. It has a bold, spicy flavor with a touch of sweetness especially in varieties where sugar or honey is added. The paste is usually sold in plastic tubs in well-stocked supermarkets and can be stored in the refrigerator for months.

Japanese pickled ginger (also known as *gari)*, is thinly sliced young ginger that has been pickled in sweet vinegar.

Served with sushi and sashimi. Pickled older ginger (*beni shoga*), usually less sweet, is also available in jars or plastic packets from Asian food stores.

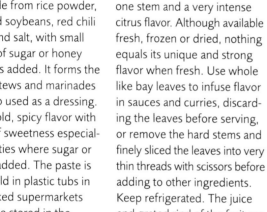

Kaffir lime leaves have an unusual double green leaf on one stem and a very intense citrus flavor. Although available fresh, frozen or dried, nothing equals its unique and strong flavor when fresh. Use whole like bay leaves to infuse flavor in sauces and curries, discarding the leaves before serving, or remove the hard stems and finely sliced the leaves into very thin threads with scissors before adding to other ingredients. Keep refrigerated. The juice and grated rind of the fruit are also used, and regular lime juice and rind can be substituted if kaffir limes are not available.

Lavash A rectangular, unleav-

ened bread, sold in packets. Ideal for wrapping foods.

Lemongrass is a fragrant lemony stalk that is either bruised and used whole in soups or curries, or sliced and ground as part of a basic spice mix. It is usually sold in bunches of stems in the supermarket. The tough outer layers should be peeled away and only the thick lower third of the stem is used. Always slice the stems before grinding to get a smooth paste.

Mirin is a gold-colored, sweet Japanese rice wine made from sake in varying strengths. Use in salads, marinades, and stir-fries. Sweet sherry or sake with a bit of sugar added both make good substitutes.

Naan is an oval-shaped unleavened Indian bread, available at some supermarkets.

To heat, follow directions on packet. Pita bread or syrian flatbread may be used as a substitute.

Nori is the Japanese term for paper-thin sheets of dried seaweed, generally used for making sushi rolls and rice balls although it is also thinly sliced and used as a garnish. Lightly toast the seaweed over an open flame before use or buy already toasted nori, known as yaki-nori, for a crisp texture. Must be kept airtight.

Palm sugar is a dense, heavy sugar made from different varieties of palm fruit. Available from Asian food stores in different shapes, sizes and colors it has a rich caramel flavor. Shave sugar off with a sharp knife. Avoid jars because the sugar becomes difficult to remove as it dries out. Dark brown sugar or maple sugar may be substituted.

Plum sauce is a tangy reddish-brown condiment made from plums, vinegar and sugar. Sold in jars or cans in Chinese stores. Other types of sweet-sour fruit jam or marmalade may be substituted.

Puff pastry is available in ready-made rolled sheets in the freezer section of most supermarkets.

Rice paper wrappers are from Vietnam and are normally sold dried. These fragile round or square wrappers are made from rice flour and water. Traditionally, batter was poured onto woven mats and then left to dry in the sun. The wrappers are soaked in warm water briefly and then used, uncooked, to wrap spring rolls. They may also be deep-fried. They are available in Asian markets.

Rice vinegar is one of the mildest vinegars available. Cider vinegar can be substituted but dilute with water as it's stronger. Rice vinegar from Japan or China is available in most good supermarkets.

Sake is a clear Japanese wine made from fermented rice. Chinese rice wine or dry sherry may be substituted.

Sambal oelek is a spicy Indonesian paste consisting of ground chili peppers, salt, palm sugar, shallots, garlic and dried shrimp paste. It can be used as a substitute for fresh chili peppers. Store in the refrigerator after opening. Any type of sweet chili paste may be used in place of it.

Sesame oil is an amber-colored aromatic oil made from toasted sesame seeds, used to add a nutty flavor to dishes at the end of cooking. Use sparingly as it is strong and store in a cool, dark cupboard.

Sesame seeds is available in Asian food stores. White sesame seeds are most commonly used. You can buy them toasted to toast them yourself in a dry frying pan over medium heat, moving them around so that they turn golden brown and do not burn. Black sesame seeds are sometimes used for sushi decoration.

Shiso leaves, also known as perilla, have a large fresh, slightly mint flavor with hints of basil. Buy fresh, green leaves. There is also a red variety that is used for coloring and flavoring umeboshi and other Japanese pickles. **Shiso powder** is made from freshly ground shiso leaves and is used as garnish or seasoning for sushi, rice or noodles.

Spring roll wrappers are very thin crepes made from wheat flour and water. Spring roll wrappers are sold frozen in packages of around 10 or 25, and are usually around 8 inches (20 cm) square or round. Available in most supermarkets. Thaw in the refrigerator before opening the package. Trim the edges of the wrappers for easier separation. Seal and store unused wrappers in the refrigerator for up to 7 days, or refreeze for up to 1 month.

Soy sauce is a salty sauce made from fermented soybeans and wheat. Sold in bottles and available in light and dark varieties; the dark is usually used in cooking and the lighter soy as a dipping sauce.

Sweet black soy sauce is a form of sweetened soy sauce that is much thicker and darker in appearance than regular soy. Use as a dipping sauce or for marinating. Also known as kecap manis.

Tamarind pulp is the soft, dried pulp of the tamarind fruit that tastes like sour prunes. Although available in powdered and liquid concentrate form, the dried pulp has better flavor. Soak the required amount in boiling water for 10 minutes, breaking it up with your fingers, then drain and discard the pulp. Used in curries, marinades and soups. Available from Asian food stores. Keep airtight and refrigerate once open. Substitute very tart fruit jam or plum sauce.

Tandoori spice paste is a classic east Indian marinade available in Indian markets. This paste is used to give foods the traditional red-orange tint of tandoor oven cooking. Tandoori paste can be rubbed directly onto the surface of meats; the powder is generally stirred into a marinade. Tandoori paste is often mixed with yogurt, minced garlic, chopped onion, lemon juice (and often ginger, as well) to make a flavorful marinade.

Thai basil has a strong, distinctive flavor, and is added to salads, sauces and stir-fries. It is widely available now, but use regular Italian basil if you cannot find it.

Thai red curry paste is a ready-made paste, made from Asian ingredients and spices. Available from most grocery stores and Asian markets. Use regular Indian curry powder mixed with chopped fresh chili peppers if you cannot find it.

Thai sweet chili sauce is a mild chili sauce with a sweet after taste. Usually used as a dipping sauce, it can also be used on burgers and barbecued meats as a marinade. Store in the refrigerator after opening. Any other type of sweet chili sauce may be substituted.

Turmeric is a root related to ginger, with a slightly bitter, pungent flavor and intense yellow-orange color. Used in Indian cooking to add flavor and color to curry dishes. Available fresh and dried from stores. Refrigerate if fresh and use ground turmeric or curry powder if fresh turmeric is unavailable.

Wasabi paste is a very hot, lime-green Japanese horseradish that is sold as a paste in a tube, which should be refrigerated once opened, or as a powder that is mixed with cold water to desired consistency. Substitute hot English or Chinese mustard.

Wonton wrappers—yellow wonton wrappers are made from an egg-based dough, while white dumpling wrappers, also called potsticker wrappers or "gow gee", are made from a wheat-based dough. Generally, the wrappers are used to make steamed or boiled dumplings. Wonton wrappers are used for boiled or fried wontons. They

are usually 3$^1/_2$ inches (9 cm) square, though they also may be round. Widely available fresh or frozen in Asian markets. Fresh wrappers will keep for up to 7 days in the refrigerator. Wrappers may be frozen.

Vietnamese mint is a spicy hot variety of mint that is delicious in salads. Also known as laksa leaf, long coriander or polygonum. Substitute a mixture of basil and coriander leaf (cilantro) if unavailable.

Cooking Equipment

The wok is a great addition to the kitchen, as it is especially suitable for steaming, stir-frying and deep-frying. Carbon-steel or rolled-steel woks—the popular, inexpensive woks found in Asian stores—are coated with a thin film of lacquer to keep them from rusting. This film needs to be removed before the wok can be used.

To remove the film of lacquer from your wok, place the wok on the stovetop. Fill with cold water, and add 2 tablespoons of baking soda (bicarbonate of soda). Bring to a boil and boil rapidly for 15 minutes. Drain, scrub off the varnish with a scouring pad, and repeat the process if any lacquer remains. Then rinse and dry the wok. It is now ready to be seasoned.

Carbon-steel, rolled-steel and cast-iron woks require seasoning before use in order to keep food from sticking to the wok and to prevent the wok from discoloring.

To season a wok, place the wok over low heat. Have a roll of paper towels and a container of oil handy. When the wok is hot, carefully wipe it with a piece of oiled paper towel. Repeat the process with fresh paper until it comes away clean and without any trace of color on it.

A seasoned wok should not be cleaned with soap, as this will remove the seasoning. To clean, use hot water and a sponge or scouring pad. Dry the wok well after washing. Store your wok in a dry, well-ventilated place. Long periods without use can cause the oil coating on the wok to become rancid. Using your wok frequently is the best way to keep this from happening.

A number of cooking utensils go hand in hand with a wok, including the bamboo steamer. Available at Asian supermarkets in a variety of sizes, these can be stacked on top of each other in a wok of simmering water, allowing the cook to prepare an entire meal at one time while using minimal electricity or gas. Bamboo steamers need only be rinsed in hot water after cooking.

A Chinese wire-mesh skimmer with a bamboo handle is perfect for removing deep-fried foods from hot oil. Long, cooking chopsticks and wooden tongs are also handy utensils for cooking Asian dishes.

A sushi mat is helpful in preparing sushi. Parchment (baking) paper is an attractive way to secure and serve bread wraps and rolls.

Dips and Sauces

Chili Lemon Dip

Serve as a dipping sauce with seafood, fish or chicken.

1 bird's-eye chili, deseeded and finely chopped
3 tablespoons fish sauce
$1/4$ cup (60 ml) fresh lime juice
1 teaspoon sesame oil
2 teaspoons grated fresh ginger

1 teaspoon shaved palm sugar or dark brown sugar
$1/4$ cup (60 ml) fresh lemon juice
$1/2$ teaspoon cracked black pepper

Combine all ingredients in a small bowl and stir until the sugar is dissolved. Store in an airtight container in the refrigerator for up to 7 days.

Makes $2/3$ cup (150 ml)

Satay Peanut Sauce

Satay Peanut Sauce

Serve as a dipping sauce with chicken, shrimp, pork or beef.

3 tablespoons smooth peanut butter
4 cloves garlic, chopped
1 teaspoon chili oil
2 tablespoons soy sauce
Pinch of salt
2 teaspoons sugar
3 tablespoons hot water
1 tablespoon hot bean paste

Combine all the ingredients and process in a food processor until smooth. Store in an airtight container in the refrigerator for up to 7 days.

Makes $3/4$ cup (180 ml)

Ginger Lime Dip

Serve as a dipping sauce with chicken or seafood.

1 tablespoon grated fresh ginger
$1/3$ cup (80 ml) fresh lime juice
2 tablespoons mirin or sweet sherry

Combine all the ingredients in a screwtop jar and shake until well combined. Store in an airtight container in the refrigerator for up to 7 days.

Makes $1/2$ cup (125 ml)

Vietnamese Chili Dip

Serve as a dipping sauce for most Asian dishes.

6 tablespoons fish sauce
2 teaspoons granulated sugar
1 tablespoon rice vinegar
2 finger-length red chili peppers, deseeded and finely chopped
1 finger-length green chili pepper, deseeded and finely chopped

Combine all the ingredients together in a small bowl and stir until the sugar is dissolved. Cover and let stand for 1 hour. Store in an airtight container in the refrigerator for up to 7 days.

Makes $\frac{1}{2}$ cup (125 ml)

Lime Soy Dip

Serve as a dipping sauce with seafood, chicken or fish.

2 tablespoons rice vinegar
2 tablespoons soy sauce
1 tablespoon fresh lime juice
1 green onion (scallion), thinly sliced

Stir all the ingredients together in a small bowl. Store in an airtight container in the refrigerator for up to 7 days.

Makes $\frac{1}{3}$ cup (80 ml)

Chili Jam (Sambal)

Use or serve as a spicy ingredient with chicken, pork, beef or seafood stir-fries.

10 finger-length dried red chili peppers
$\frac{1}{3}$ cup (80 ml) oil
1 red bell pepper, deseeded, deribbed, and chopped
Cloves from 1 head garlic, coarsely chopped
15 shallots, peeled and chopped
$\frac{1}{2}$ cup (90 g) shaved palm sugar or dark brown sugar
2 tablespoons tamarind pulp

1 Put the dried chili peppers in a bowl and add enough boiling water to cover. Let stand for 15 minutes or until softened. Drain, deseed and chop the chilies. In a food processor, combine the chilies, oil, bell pepper, garlic and shallots. Blend until smooth, about 30 seconds.
2 In a wok or skillet over medium heat, cook the chili mixture, stirring constantly, for 15 minutes. Add the palm sugar and tamarind pulp. Reduce the heat to low and simmer for 10 minutes or until the mixture darkens and thickens to a jam-like consistency. Store in a sterilized jar in the refrigerator for up to 3 months.

Makes $\frac{1}{2}$ cup (125 ml)

Vietnamese Chili Dip

Spiced Bar Nuts

One of the easiest ways to keep hungry guests at bay is with a flavorful nut mix. This delicious combination of cashews, almonds and peanuts, made slightly zesty with Indian spices, is an exciting twist on the standard nut mix that will add spice to any party!

3 tablespoons oil
1 cup (150 g) raw cashew nuts
1 cup (150 g) blanched whole almonds
1 cup (150 g) raw peanuts
1 tablespoon salt
1 teaspoon garam masala
$^1/_2$ teaspoon ground red pepper (cayenne)

Makes 3 cups (470 g)

1 In a wok or skillet, heat the oil over medium heat. Add the cashew nuts and cook, stirring constantly, until lightly browned, 1–2 minutes. Using a slotted spoon, transfer them to paper towels to drain. Repeat to fry the almonds, then the peanuts.
2 Combine the nuts in a medium bowl. Add the remaining ingredients and stir until well combined. Serve at room temperature.

Note: These tasty little morsels make a great snack to serve with drinks.

Yogurt Mango Dip

This simple yet delicious dip takes minutes to make, and is the perfect quick hunger fix.

1 tablespoon oil
1 onion, finely chopped
1 teaspoon mild curry powder
1$^1/_4$ cups (300 ml) plain yogurt
2 tablespoons mango chutney
Mixed fresh vegetables and pita chips or
   baby pappadams, for serving

Serves 4–6

1 Heat the oil in a small frying pan over medium heat. Add the onion and cook until softened, about 1 minute. Stir in the curry powder and cook until aromatic, about 1 minute. Remove the pan from the heat and allow to cool.

2 Gently stir in the yogurt and mango chutney. Spoon into a serving bowl, place in the center of a platter and surround with vegetables such as Belgian endive (*chicory*) leaves, slices of carrot, celery, red and green bell peppers, English (hothouse) cucumber, blanched cauliflower florets and blanched asparagus spears. If desired, fry the pappadams in hot oil or microwave on high according to directions on package.

Note: Dip can be made 1 day ahead. Keep covered and refrigerated for up to 3 or 4 days.

Soy Glazed Chicken Drummettes

Marinated in a flavorful Chinese-inspired barbecue sauce, these tender and finger-licking-good Chicken Drummettes are a well-loved alternative to the ubiquitous buffalo-style chicken wings, which tend to be fiery hot without a lot of flavor. Alternatively, the drummettes can barbecued on a gas or charcoal grill.

24 small chicken wings
2 tablespoons oil
3 tablespoons hoisin sauce
4 tablespoons soy sauce
2 tablespoons dry sherry or sake
4 cloves garlic, crushed
1 red finger-length chili pepper, deseeded
   and chopped (optional)
3 teaspoons grated fresh ginger
Hoisin sauce or sweet black soy sauce, for
   dipping

Makes 24 drummettes

1 Cut the chicken wings in half at the main joint. Discard the wing tips (or reserve them for making stock). With a sharp knife, trim the meat around each cut joint, then scrape the meat down the bone and push it over the bottom joint so that the wing resembles a small chicken leg. Place the drummettes in a shallow dish.
2 Combine the oil, 3 tablespoons hoisin sauce, soy sauce, sherry, garlic, chili (if using) and ginger in a screw-top jar. Shake until well combined. Pour over the chicken. Cover and marinate in the refrigerator for 3 hours.
3 Preheat oven to 350°F (180°C). Remove the chicken from the marinade and place them in a lightly greased baking dish. Bake in the preheated oven until tender, 15–20 minutes.
4 Serve hot or cold, with the hoisin sauce or sweet black soy sauce for dipping.

Chili and Herb Shrimp

These subtly flavored shrimp are enhanced with the delicate and lemony-fresh aroma of lemongrass, which goes beautifully with any type of fish or seafood.

4 lbs (2 kg) fresh jumbo shrimp
$1/_3$ cup (80 ml) olive oil
2 tablespoons chopped fresh ginger
2 cloves garlic, crushed
2 stalks lemongrass, inner part of bottom
  third only, crushed or a pinch of lemon rind
1 red finger-length chili pepper, deseeded
  and chopped
2 limes or lemons, juiced
$1/_4$ cup (10 g) chopped mixed fresh herbs
2 tablespoons oil
Lime or lemon wedges, to garnish

1 Peel and devein the shrimp.
2 Combine the $1/_3$ cup olive oil, ginger, garlic, lemongrass, chili pepper, lime juice and herbs in a large bowl. Mix well. Add the shrimp and toss until well coated in the marinade. Cover with plastic wrap and refrigerate for 1 hour.
3 Warm the 2 tablespoons of oil in a frying pan over medium heat. Drain the shrimp. Working in batches, fry the shrimp until they just change color, 2–3 minutes. Serve immediately with lime or lemon wedges and toothpicks on the side, or thread on skewers as shown.

Serves 10

Chicken Yakitori Skewers

In this classic Japanese style of barbecue, chicken is marinated in a delicious sauce and then lightly grilled on bamboo skewers. To make a vegetarian version, use firm or extra-firm tofu in place of the chicken. Press the tofu under a weight to release moisture before adding it to the marinade.

$1/_2$ cup (125 ml) soy sauce
$1/_2$ cup (125 ml) sake or dry sherry
2 teaspoons sugar
1 tablespoon grated fresh ginger
2 tablespoons snipped chives
$1^1/_2$ lbs (700 g) boneless chicken breast fillets
12 green onions (scallions), dark green tops
  removed, cut into lengths
10 bamboo skewers, soaked in water for 10
  minutes, then drained
Oil, for brushing
Soy sauce, for dipping

1 Place the soy sauce, sake, sugar, ginger and chives in a screw-top jar and shake well to mix.
2 Trim the chicken breasts of any fat and membranes and cut into bite-sized cubes, about $1^1/_2$ inches (4 cm). Place the chicken cubes in a shallow glass or ceramic dish, pour the marinade over the cubes, cover and refrigerate for 1 hour.
3 Preheat a broiler (grill) or charcoal grill. Drain the chicken and thread the cubes onto skewers alternately with the green onions. Brush with the olive oil and cook until golden, about 5 minutes per side. Serve hot with the soy sauce for dipping.

Serves 10

Classsic Chinese Spring Rolls

When you're saving room for dinner (or more mouth-watering finger foods!), a big meaty egg roll can be too much. At those times, the smaller spring roll is perfect. In China these delicate rolls are traditionally served on the first day of the New Year, in early spring. I like them year-round.

18 square spring roll wrappers (8 by 8 inches/
   20 by 20 cm), thawed
1 egg white, lightly beaten
Oil, for deep-frying
Bottled sweet and sour sauce or Thai sweet
   chili sauce, for dipping

Filling
2 tablespoons oil
3 cloves garlic, chopped
2 tablespoons grated fresh ginger
$1^1/_2$ cups (300 g) ground pork or chicken
$1/_4$ cup (65 g) fresh shrimp meat, finely
   chopped
2 celery sticks, finely chopped
1 carrot, peeled and grated
6 green onions (scallions), finely chopped
1 cup (100 g) shredded Chinese (Napa)
   cabbage
2 teaspoons fish sauce
$1/_2$ teaspoon salt
$1/_2$ teaspoon ground pepper
1 cup (50 g) fresh bean sprouts

Makes 18 rolls

1 To make the Filling, heat 1 tablespoon of the oil in a wok or large skillet and stir-fry the garlic and ginger for 1 minute or until fragrant. Add the ground pork or chicken, and shrimp meat. Stir-fry for 3 minutes or until cooked. Transfer to a bowl and set aside.
2 Wipe the wok and heat the remaining 1 tablespoon of oil. Add the celery, carrot, green onions and cabbage. Stir-fry for 2 minutes or until the cabbage softens. Add the fish sauce, salt, pepper and the meat mixture. Remove from the heat. Stir in the bean sprouts and mix well. Let cool completely.
3 Place 1 spring roll wrapper on a clean work surface. Brush the edges of the wrapper with some of the egg white. Place 2 heaping tablespoonfuls of the Filling in the center of the wrapper. Roll the bottom of the wrapper diagonally over the filling. Fold in the sides and roll up diagonally. Seal the edges with some egg white. Repeat with the remaining wrappers and filling to make more rolls.
4 In a large wok, heat the oil to 375°F (190°C) or until a small bread cube dropped in the oil sizzles and turns golden. Fry the spring rolls in batches until golden, about 2 minutes. Using a slotted spoon, transfer the fried rolls to paper towels to drain. Serve hot, with the sweet and sour sauce or Thai sweet chili sauce.

Crisp Asparagus Wraps

This elegant appetizer adds panache to any gathering, and is the ultimate finger food—one hand for an aperitif and one for an Asparagus Wasabi Wrap.

12 asparagus spears, trimmed

48 square wonton wrappers (3¹/₂ by 3¹/₂ inches/9 by 9 cm)

About 1 tablespoon wasabi paste or hot English mustard

Oil, for deep-frying

Makes 24 wraps

1 Cut each asparagus spear in half crosswise.

2 Place 2 wonton wrappers on a clean work surface (keep the remaining wrappers covered with a damp cloth to prevent from drying out). Lightly spread 1 wrapper with a little wasabi paste or mustard. Place the second wrapper on top. Place 1 piece of the asparagus diagonally across one corner of the stacked wrappers. Brush the edges with water. Roll the asparagus in the wrappers, allowing one end of the asparagus to protrude.

3 In a large wok, heat the oil to 375°F (190°C) or until a small bread cube dropped in the oil sizzles and turns golden. Add the wraps in batches and fry until golden, about 2 minutes. Using a slotted spoon, transfer the wraps to paper towels to drain. Serve hot.

Meatballs with Fresh Basil and Sweet Chili Sauce

Meatballs are such a classic party food. We've all run across a Swedish, Hungarian or Italian meatball at a buffet table or holiday party in our lifetimes. Why not surprise your guests with these spicy, Thai-inspired meatballs flavored with aromatic red curry paste and fresh herbs?

8 oz (250 g) ground pork
3 teaspoons Thai red curry paste
2 cloves garlic, finely chopped
1 tablespoon chopped Thai basil leaves
2 tablespoons chopped coriander leaves
  (cilantro)
2 bird's-eye chilies, deseeded and chopped
1 teaspoon soy sauce
$1/4$ cup (15 g) bread crumbs
Oil, for deep frying
12 large fresh basil or shiso leaves
Thai sweet chili sauce, for dipping

1 In a medium bowl, combine the pork, curry paste, garlic, basil, coriander leaves, chilies, soy sauce and bread crumbs. Using wet hands, mix until well combined. Divide into 12 portions and shape each portion into a ball.
2 Heat the oil in a wok or large skillet over medium heat and fry the pork balls in batches until browned, 2–3 minutes. Using a slotted spoon, transfer to paper towels to drain. Let cool for 10 minutes.
3 Wrap each pork ball in a basil or shiso leaf and secure with a toothpick. Serve hot, with the chili sauce for dipping.

Makes 12 meatballs

Bite-sized Chinese Shrimp Toasts

These delicious and pretty shrimp toasts, with a tantalizingly crusty exterior, are the perfect bite-sized party food. (And I can't think of a better way to use up stale sandwich bread—especially if you don't live near a duck pond.) For variety, try these toasts with scallops instead of shrimp.

12 large slices stale white sandwich bread
2 green onions (scallions), chopped
2 cloves garlic, crushed
1 teaspoon grated fresh ginger
8 oz (250 g) fresh shrimp, peeled and
  deveined
1 tablespoon cornstarch
1 teaspoon soy sauce
2 tablespoons chopped fresh coriander
  leaves (cilantro)
1 egg yolk
2 teaspoons sesame seeds
Oil, for deep-frying

Makes 24 pieces

1 Using a 2-inch (5-cm) cookie (pastry) cutter, cut 2 rounds from each slice of bread. Place the green onions, garlic, ginger, shrimp, cornstarch, soy sauce and coriander leaves in a food processor. Process until the mixture forms a thick paste, about 15 seconds. Brush one side of each bread round with the egg yolk, then spread with 1 teaspoon of the shrimp mixture. Sprinkle with the sesame seeds.

2 Heat the oil in a deep, heavy-bottomed saucepan or a wok until it reaches 375°F (190°C) or until a small cube of bread dropped into the oil sizzles and turns golden. Working in batches, deep-fry the bread rounds in the hot oil until golden and crisp on both sides, 1–2 minutes total. Remove the bread rounds and drain on paper towels. Serve immediately.

Note: The shrimp mixture can be prepared 2 hours ahead. Keep the mixture covered and refrigerated.

Baked Vegetable Samosas with Mint

Called turnovers in the West, this Indian version is made with a signature spice and fresh herb combination.

3 large potatoes, peeled and chopped
$^2/_3$ cup (100 g) cooked green peas
1 teaspoon cumin seeds
1–2 green finger-length chilies, deseeded
  and finely chopped
$^1/_2$ red onion, finely chopped
3 tablespoons chopped fresh coriander
  leaves (cilantro)
2 tablespoons chopped fresh mint leaves
$^1/_3$ cup (80 ml) fresh lemon juice
12 sheets frozen filo pastry, thawed
$^1/_3$ cup (80 ml) oil

Makes 12 samosas

1 Preheat oven to 400°F (200°C). Line a baking tray with parchment paper. Cook the potatoes in salted boiling water until tender, about 8 minutes. Drain and mash. In a medium bowl, combine the mashed potatoes with the rest of the ingredients. Stir until well combined.
2 Place 1 sheet of the filo pastry on a clean work surface (keep remaining filo covered with a damp cloth). Brush lightly with oil. Fold in half lengthwise. Brush again with oil. Place 1 heaping tablespoonful of the potato filling at one end of the pastry strip. Fold the corner over the filling to make a triangle. Continue folding in the same fashion to make a triangular package. Place on the prepared pan. Brush with oil. Repeat to make more samosas. Bake for 15–20 minutes or until golden and crisp. Serve hot.

Shrimp Nuggets with Herbs

These "poppers" go down so easy that you'll have trouble getting them out of the fryer quick enough!

8 oz (250 g) fresh shrimp, shelled, deveined and chopped
$1/2$ onion, finely chopped
3 cloves garlic, finely chopped
2 teaspoons grated fresh ginger
2 tablespoons chopped coriander leaves
1 finger-length red chili pepper, deseeded and finely chopped
$1/2$ teaspoon ground cumin
$1/2$ teaspoon garam masala
2 tablespoons chickpea flour
2 tablespoons all-purpose (plain) flour
Oil, for deep-frying

1 In a medium bowl, combine the shrimp, onion, garlic, ginger, coriander leaves, chili, cumin and garam masala. Stir until well combined. Divide into 8 portions and shape into nuggets.
2 Combine the two types of flour in a big bowl. Roll the nuggets in the combined flours.
3 In a wok, or deep fryer, heat the oil to 375°F (190°C) or until a small bread cube dropped in the oil sizzles and turns golden in 1 minute. Add the shrimp nuggets in batches and fry for 2–3 minutes or until golden. Using a slotted spoon, transfer the nuggets to paper towels to drain. Serve immediately, with the lime wedges on the side.

Makes 8 nuggets

Roast Duck Rolls with Sweet Hoisin Sauce

These no-fuss rolls combine two Chinese favorites: succulent, flavorful duck meat and hoisin sauce. If you don't live near an Asian market that offers fresh-roasted duck meat, and don't want to roast a duck at home, use dark meat from a roast turkey (a great way to enjoy Thanksgiving leftovers). Or, easier yet, use dark meat from a store-bought rotisserie chicken.

1 Chinese roast duck (purchased from a
  Chinese takeaway)
12 green onions (scallions)
4 carrots, peeled and finely sliced
4 flour tortillas or flatbread or chapati
48 toothpicks
Hoisin sauce, for dipping

Note: Prepare the duck, green onions and carrots 2 hours ahead. Assemble just before serving.

Makes about 48 rolls

1 Remove the meat from the duck and discard the bones. Slice the meat and skin into bite-sized pieces.
2 Trim away the root ends of the green onions, then cut them into $1^1/_4$-inch (3-cm) lengths. Using a sharp knife or kitchen shears, make $^1/_4$-inch (6-mm) cuts in each green onion, forming a fringe. Place the green onion brushes in a bowl of ice water (green onions will curl in ice water). Place the carrots in the bowl of ice water with the green onions. Chill until ready to serve.
3 Warm the tortillas in a microwave oven for 1 minute or wrapped in aluminum foil in a 275°F (140°C) oven for 10 minutes. Using kitchen shears, cut the tortillas into $^3/_4$-inch by 4-inch (2-cm by 10-cm) strips.
4 Working in batches, place the tortilla strips on a clean work surface. Top each strip with a small amount of duck, 1 green onion brush, 4 to 5 carrot pieces and a dash of hoisin sauce. Roll up and secure with a toothpick.
5 Serve with hoisin sauce for dipping.

Warm Tandoori Chicken Wraps

This Indian-spiced wrap is inspired by the classic pairing of tandoori chicken and naan—a traditional flat bread. Why not combine the two in an easy-to-hold wrap? Tandoori paste, composed of a complex assortment of aromatic spices, gets its red-orange tint from ground annatto seed, though food coloring is sometimes added to less authentic blends.

$1/3$ cup (80 ml) plain tandoori spice paste

2 tablespoons plus $1/2$ cup (125 ml) yogurt

Grated rind and juice of 1 lemon

3 skinless, boneless chicken breasts

2 carrots, peeled

1 English (hothouse) cucumber or green bell pepper, halved and deseeded, sliced into thin strips

6 pieces naan or syrian flatbread

1 clove garlic, finely chopped

Leaves from 6 fresh mint sprigs, plus 2 tablespoons finely chopped fresh mint leaves

Makes 6 wraps

1 In a small bowl, combine the tandoori paste, 2 tablespoons yogurt, lemon rind and lemon juice. Put the chicken in a baking dish. Pour the tandoori mixture over and stir until the chicken is well coated. Cover and refrigerate for 2 hours.

2 Heat a grill pan or oven broiler. Brush the grill or pan lightly with oil. Cook the chicken for 4–5 minutes on each side or until the juices run clear when pierced with a skewer. Transfer to a cutting board and let rest for 5 minutes. Cut each tenderloin into 2 long strips (if using chicken breast fillets, slice each fillet into 4 long strips).

3 Using a vegetable peeler, cut the carrot into thin ribbons. To heat the naan or flatbread, follow the instructions on the packet. In a small bowl, stir the $1/2$ cup yogurt, garlic and chopped mint leaves together.

4 Place the bread on a clean work surface. Divide the chicken, cucumber, carrot and mint leaves among the naan. Drizzle with the yogurt mixture. Wrap the naan around the filling and serve immediately.

Beef Tataki Slices with Wasabi Soy Dip

This delicate Japanese dish is a favorite among meat lovers—it's all about the meat! Traditionally the meat is quickly seared over a hot flame (usually a grill) to leave to juicy, tender and raw interior—think steak tartare. You can also blanch the beef for a short 10 seconds, though either method can be used.

1 white onion, finely sliced
2 green onions (scallions), finely chopped
10 oz (300 g) tender beef sirloin
Green leaves such as bamboo or camelia, for decoration
$1/2$ cup (75 g) grated red radish
Wasabi paste and soy sauce, for dipping

Vinegar Mixture
$1/2$ cup (125 ml) rice vinegar or white vinegar
1 teaspoon mirin or sweet sherry
1 tablespoon sugar

1 Combine all the Vinegar Mixture ingredients in a bowl. Stir well until the sugar is dissolved. Add the onion and green onion.
2 Bring a saucepan of water to a boil. Blanch the beef for 10 seconds. Remove the beef from the saucepan and add to the Vinegar Mixture while the beef is still hot; toss well. Refrigerate for 30 minutes. Remove the marinated beef from the Mixture and sliced thinly. Arrange the slices in a flower shape on a plate with the marinated white onion slices and chopped green onion in the center. Garnish with the green leaves. Serve with the wasabi and soy sauce for dipping. Accompany with grated radish in a side plate.

Serves 4

Thai Fish Cakes

These enticing fish cakes, bursting with the signature Thai flavors of citrus, fresh coriander, zesty red curry paste and essential fish sauce, can be made with any type of mild- to moderate-flavored fish fillets.

1 lb (500 g) boneless fresh fish fillets
1 tablespoon Thai red curry paste
1 tablespoon fish sauce
1 egg, beaten
2 teaspoons brown sugar
1 clove garlic, crushed
2 teaspoons grated lime rind
2 tablespoons chopped coriander leaves
2 green onions (scallions), finely sliced
1/2 cup (75 g) finely sliced green beans
3 tablespoons oil, for frying
Soy sauce, for dipping

1 Place the fish fillets, curry paste, fish sauce, egg, sugar and garlic in a food processor. Process until the mixture forms a thick paste, about 20 seconds. Transfer to a bowl. Add the lime rind, coriander leaves, green onions and beans. Using wet hands, mix until well combined. Form the mixture into 36 balls. Flatten each ball to form a patty.
2 Heat the oil in a frying pan over medium heat. Working in batches, fry the fish cakes until golden, about 1 minute on each side. Remove and drain on paper towels. Serve with the soy sauce for dipping and fresh lime wedges, threading the fish cakes on skewers as shown if desired.

Makes 36 cakes

Baked Chicken Puffs

Tied up like pretty packages, these Baked Chicken Puffs are hard to resist. Slightly sweet and spicy, these delicious stuffed pockets are accented with the bright flavors of scallions and fresh herbs and are served with a tangy-tart Lemon Chili Dip.

1 tablespoon oil

4 cloves garlic, finely chopped

1 bird's-eye chili, deseeded and finely chopped

7 oz (200 g) ground chicken

3 tablespoons bottled sweet and sour sauce or Thai sweet chili sauce

2 teaspoons fish sauce

1 tablespoon chopped fresh Thai basil

2 tablespoons chopped fresh coriander leaves (cilantro)

Salt and freshly ground pepper to taste

5 green onions (scallions)

5 frozen puff pastry sheets, thawed

1 egg, beaten

Chili Lemon Dip (page 16) or soy sauce, for dipping

1 Heat the oil in a wok over medium heat and stir-fry the garlic and chili for 1 minute or until fragrant. Add the chicken and stir-fry until opaque, about 3 minutes. Remove from the heat. Stir in the sweet and sour or chili sauce, fish sauce, basil, coriander leaves, salt and pepper. Mix well. Let cool completely.

2 Meanwhile, cut each green onion into 4 pieces lengthwise. Put in a bowl and add enough boiling water to cover. Let stand for 1 minute. Drain and rinse under cold running water. Drain again.

3 Preheat oven to 425°F (220°C). Line 2 baking trays with parchment (baking) paper. Using a $1/4$-inch (6-mm) cutter, cut the puff pastry into 20 rounds. Spoon 2–3 teaspoonfuls of the chicken filling onto the center of each round. Brush the edges of each round with the beaten egg. Fold the pastry over the filling to form a semicircle and press the edges firmly together. Tie a green onion length around each puff. Place on prepared paper. Brush with the beaten egg.

4 Bake until golden and crisp, 12–15 minutes. Serve warm, with the Lemon Chili Dip or soy sauce.

Makes 20 puffs

Bite-sized Spring Rolls with Pork and Basil

These pork and basil rolls will tempt your guests with the distinctive and delicious flavors of Southeast Asia. And, easy to down in two bites, these petite spring rolls are a perfect finger food for parties (one hand for a refreshing libation; one hand for a tasty nibble).

Handful of dried cellophane noodles
4 oz (125 g) ground pork
2 cloves garlic, finely chopped
2 teaspoons grated fresh ginger
1 tablespoon finely chopped Thai basil
1 tablespoon finely chopped coriander leaves
  (cilantro)
1 bird's-eye chili, deseeded and finely chopped
1 teaspoon soy sauce
6 dried rice paper wrappers (8 inches/
  20 cm) in diameter
1 egg, beaten
Oil, for deep-frying
Vietnamese Chili Dip (page 17)

Makes about 32 rolls

1 Put the noodles in a heatproof bowl and add enough boiling water to cover. Let soak for 10 minutes. Drain. Using scissors, coarsely cut the noodles into shorter lengths. In a medium bowl, combine the noodles, pork, garlic, ginger, basil, coriander leaves, chili and soy sauce. Using wet hands, mix until well combined.
2 Using scissors, cut the rice paper wrappers into quarters. Working in batches, brush each wrapper quarter with the beaten egg. Let stand for 2–3 minutes or until softened. Place 1 heaping teaspoonful of the pork mixture near the rounded end of each wrapper quarter. Fold the rounded end over the filling, fold in the sides and roll into a small cylinder. Repeat with the remaining wrappers and filling.
3 In a deep fryer or wok, heat the oil until smoking. Working with 4–6 pork rolls at a time, deep-fry until golden and crisp, 3–4 minutes. Using a slotted spoon, transfer to paper towels to drain. Serve hot, with the dipping sauce.

1 Working in batches, brush each wrapper with beaten egg. Allow to stand 2–3 minutes or until softened.

2 Place 1 heaping teaspoonful of the pork filling near the rounded end of each wrapper quarter.

3 Fold the rounded end of the wrapper over the filling. Fold in the sides and roll into a small cylinder.

Fresh Thai Spring Rolls

These light rolls are fresh, fresh, fresh!—the perfect appetizer for a backyard gathering on a warm spring or summer evening. Served chilled, Fresh Thai Spring Rolls—sometimes called summer or salad rolls—are filled with flavorful crisp vegetables, fresh herbs and just-cooked shrimp.

Handful of dried cellophane noodles
$1/2$ cup (75 g) finely sliced carrot
$1/2$ cup (75 g) finely sliced zucchini
$1/2$ cup (75 g) finely sliced red bell pepper
6 green onions (scallions), finely sliced
Juice of 1 lime
2 tablespoons fish sauce
1 teaspoon grated fresh ginger
$1/4$ cup (10 g) chopped coriander leaves
2 tablespoons Thai sweet chili sauce
$1/4$ cup (10 g) whole coriander leaves (cilantro)
16 dried rice paper wrappers, 6 inches
   (15 cm) in diameter
16 cooked jumbo shrimp (king prawns),
   peeled and deveined
16 garlic chives
Thai sweet chili sauce or soy sauce,
   for dipping

1 Place the cellophane noodles in a bowl and cover with boiling water. Allow to stand until softened, about 10 minutes, then drain.
2 In a bowl, combine the carrot, zucchini, bell pepper, green onions, lime juice, fish sauce, ginger and chopped coriander leaves. Allow to stand for 10 minutes. Drain well, then place in a bowl. Add the chili sauce and coriander leaves and mix well.
3 Fill a bowl with warm water and place a paper towel on a clean work surface. Dip a rice paper wrapper in the hot water until soft, about 15 seconds, then place on the paper towel. Spoon 1 table-spoon of the vegetable mixture onto the center of the wrapper, top with a small amount of noodles, a shrimp and a garlic chive (allow the chive to protrude above the wrapper's edge), then roll the wrapper into a cylinder. Cover the prepared rolls with a damp kitchen towel to prevent them from drying out. Repeat with the remaining ingredients.
4 Serve with the Thai sweet chili sauce or soy sauce for dipping.

Makes 16

1 Dip one rice paper wrapper at a time into a bowl of hot water to soften them.

2 Spoon a small amount of filling onto the middle of each wrapper.

3 Fold edges over and roll up. Cover rolls with a damp towel until ready to serve.

Baked Tandoori Chicken Pieces

This hearty and finger-licking-good appetizer is extremely flexible. Along with thigh and leg pieces, you can use smaller wing pieces, though remember not to cook them as long. If you have a grill with a lid, you can barbecue the pieces (with the lid closed) instead of bake them. The choice is yours.

4 chicken legs and thighs
$^3/_4$ cup (180 ml) plain yogurt
1 teaspoon garam masala
2 teaspoons grated fresh ginger
6 cloves garlic, finely chopped
$^1/_4$ teaspoon ground turmeric
1 teaspoon ground coriander
1 tablespoon fresh lemon juice
$^1/_4$ teaspoon Chinese powdered red food coloring (optional)
Pinch of salt
1 tablespoon oil
2 limes, quartered

Serves 4

1 Using a sharp knife, separate the drumsticks from the thighs and make 2 slits in the skin side of each chicken piece. Place the chicken pieces in a baking dish. In a small bowl, combine the yogurt, garam masala, ginger, garlic, turmeric, coriander, lemon juice, red coloring (if using), salt and oil. Mix well. Pour over the chicken pieces and toss to coat the chicken. Cover and refrigerate for 2 hours.

2 Remove the chicken from the refrigerator 30 minutes before roasting. Preheat oven to 425°F (220°C). Transfer the chicken to a roasting pan. Roast for 25 minutes or until the juices run clear when the chicken is pierced with a sharp knife. Remove from the oven. Serve immediately, with the lime wedges on the side.

Note: Tandoori chicken is traditionally cooked on a spit in a clay tandoor oven, but you can also prepare it in a regular oven or on a grill.

Baked Pork Roll-ups

Hail to modern conveniences! This easy recipe is the perfect blend of great flavor, impressive good looks, and an incredible time saver—frozen puff pastry. Sambal oelek—a spicy Indonesian paste—gives these tasty roll-ups their distinctive flavor, and will keep your guests pining for more.

3 green onion (scallion leaves), halved
  lengthwise
6 oz (185 g) ground pork
2 teaspoons sambal oelek
3 cloves garlic, finely chopped
$1/4$ cup (10 g) finely chopped fresh coriander
  leaves (cilantro)
$1/4$ teaspoon salt
$1/4$ teaspoon ground white pepper
1 sheet frozen puff pastry, thawed
1 egg, beaten
Soy sauce for dipping

Makes about 16 rolls

1 Put the green onions in a bowl and add enough boiling water to cover. Let stand for 1 minute. Drain and rinse under cold running water.

2 Preheat oven to 450°F (230°C). Line a baking tray with parchment (baking) paper.

3 In a bowl, combine the pork, sambal oelek, garlic, coriander leaves, salt and pepper. Put the puff pastry on a clean work surface and cut into 4 rectangles. Place a line of pork mixture down the center of each pastry piece. Brush the edges of the pastry with the beaten egg. Fold the long ends of each pastry over the pork filling, overlapping slightly and sealing to form a neat sausage roll. Trim away any excess pastry. Cut each roll, crosswise, into pieces 1-inch (2.5-cm) wide.

4 Place on the prepared pan, sealed side down. Brush the tops with the beaten egg. Tie a green onion around each piece. Brush each piece again with the beaten egg. Bake until golden and crisp, about 15 minutes. Remove from the oven and serve hot, with the soy sauce for dipping.

Bite-sized Oyster Rolls with Soy Lime Dip

These oyster rolls are such a treat. Whereas raw oysters are not universally appreciated, cooked oysters, in one form or another, are loved worldwide. Subtly flavored with Asian seasonings, this rich roll is perfectly balanced with the refreshingly acidic Soy Lime Dip.

2 tablespoons grated fresh ginger
1 tablespoon chopped coriander leaves
  (cilantro)
1 tablespoon finely chopped green onions
  (scallions)
1 teaspoon grated lime rind
1 teaspoon fresh lime juice
1 teaspoon sesame oil
24 square wonton wrapper
24 fresh oysters
Oil, for deep-frying
Soy Lime Dip (page 17)

Makes 24 rolls

1 In a small bowl, combine the ginger, coriander leaves, green onion, lime rind and juice and sesame oil. Stir until well combined.
2 Place 1 wonton wrapper on a clean work surface with the corner facing towards you (keep the remaining wrappers covered with a damp cloth to prevent from drying out). Place 1 oyster diagonally across the bottom corner of the wrapper. Spoon about $1/2$ teaspoonful of the ginger mixture on top of the oyster. Brush the edges with water. Fold the bottom corner of the wrapper over the oyster. Fold in the sides and roll. Cover with a damp cloth and repeat with the remaining wrappers and filling.
3 In a wok or a deep fryer, heat the oil until smoking. Working in batches, fry the oyster rolls until golden, about 2 minutes. Using a slotted spoon, transfer the rolls to paper towels to drain. Serve hot, with the Soy Lime Dip.

1 Place a wonton wrapper on a clean work surface with one end facing you, keep remaining wrappers covered with a damp cloth.

2 Place 1 oyster $1/2$ inch (12 mm) from end of the wrapper. Spoon about $1/2$ teaspoonful of the ginger mixture on top of the oyster.

3 Brush the edges of the wrapper with water. Fold the bottom of the wrapper over the oyster. Fold in the sides and roll up.

Steamed Shrimp and Spinach Dumplings

These beautiful translucent dumplings have a delicate texture that nearly melts in your mouth. Once you've mastered the basic technique of making steamed dumplings, try different filling combinations. In place of spinach, for example, try another quick cooking green such as watercress or Swiss chard.

8 oz (250 g) fresh shrimp or prawns, peeled and deveined, finely chopped
1 tablespoon oil
2 cloves garlic, crushed
1 cup (30 g) spinach leaves, washed and finely sliced
2 tablespoons finely chopped canned water chestnuts
2 green onions (scallions), finely chopped
1 tablespoon soy sauce
16 fresh or frozen wonton wrappers
Soy sauce or Thai sweet chili sauce, for dipping

Note: Dumpling filling can be prepared 2 hours ahead. Keep covered and refrigerated.

Makes 16 dumplings

1 Heat the oil in a wok or frying pan over medium heat. Add the garlic and fry until aromatic, about 1 minute. Stir in the spinach and chopped shrimp and stir-fry until the shrimp change color, about 2 minutes. Remove from the heat and allow to cool. Add the water chestnuts, green onions and soy sauce to the shrimp and spinach mixture. Mix until well combined.

2 Place the wonton wrappers on a clean work surface and cover with a damp kitchen towel. Working with one wrapper at a time, lay the wrapper on the work surface and place 1 teaspoon of the shrimp filling in the middle. Brush the edges of the wonton wrapper with water (use a pastry brush or a finger). Gather the dumpling corners together and twist to seal. Set aside and cover with plastic wrap. Repeat with the remaining wonton wrappers and shrimp filling.

3 Place the dumplings in a steamer or steamer basket lined with parchment (baking) paper, leaving some space for steam to circulate efficiently. Partially fill a wok or pot with water (steamer or basket should not touch the water) and bring to a rapid boil. Place the steamer over the boiling water and cover. Steam for 12 minutes, adding more water to the wok if necessary. Lift the steamer off the wok and carefully remove the dumplings.

4 Serve warm with the Thai sweet chili sauce or soy sauce for dipping.

Crisp Shrimp Rolls with Sweet Sour Sauce

In these decadent crispy-fried rolls butterflied shrimp are stuffed with a flavorful mixture of ground pork, fresh coriander, soy sauce and ginger. Served with a tangy sweet and sour dipping sauce, these shrimp rolls are a tried-and-true party favorite.

12 fresh shrimp or prawns, shelled (tails intact)

12 frozen spring roll wrappers (8 by 8 inches/ 20 by 20 cm), thawed

1 egg white, lightly beaten

Oil, for deep-frying

2 lime wedges for serving

Bottled sweet and sour sauce or Thai sweet chili sauce, for dipping

Filling

4 oz (125 g) ground pork

2 cloves garlic, finely chopped

1 teaspoon grated fresh ginger

1 tablespoon chopped coriander leaves (cilantro)

1 green onion (scallion), finely chopped

1 teaspoon soy sauce

Makes 12 wraps

1 Make the Filling by combining the pork, garlic, ginger, coriander leaves, green onion and soy sauce in a bowl. Mix until well combined. Set aside.

2 Cut halfway through the back of each shrimp. Remove the dark vein from each shrimp and open the shrimp flat. Spread about 1–2 teaspoons of the Filling on one side of each shrimp. Press the shrimp sides back together.

3 Place 1 spring roll wrapper on a clean work surface. Fold the wrapper in half diagonally. Brush the wrapper surface with the egg white. Place a shrimp on the wrapper 1 inch (2.5 cm) from the end, allowing its tail to overhang edge of the wrapper. Roll the bottom of the wrapper over the shrimp, leaving the shrimp tail unwrapped. Fold in the sides and roll up. Again, leave the shrimp tail unwrapped. Cover with plastic wrap and repeat with remaining ingredients.

4 In a wok or a deep fryer, heat the oil to 375°F (190°C) or until a small cube of bread dropped in the oil sizzles and turns golden. Working with 2 shrimp wraps at a time, deep-fry them until golden and crisp, 3–4 minutes. Using a slotted spoon, transfer to paper towels to drain. Serve hot, with the lime wedges and sweet and sour sauce or Thai sweet chili sauce as a dip.

Barbecued Pork Rolls with Plum Sauce

Easy to make and extremely versatile—you can pass these barbecued pork rolls at a party (as a firmly grasped two-handed nosh), serve them as a starter or enjoy them as snack between meals.

1 tablespoon plum sauce
1 tablespoon orange juice
1 teaspoon soy sauce
1 tablespoon oil
3 cloves garlic, finely chopped
1 finger-length red chili pepper, deseeded
  and sliced
2 cups (150 g) bok choy, cut into lengths
8 oz (250 g) Chinese barbecued pork, sliced
4 pieces lavash or flour tortillas
$1/4$ cup (15 g) fried noodles (flour sticks)
2 tablespoons Crispy Fried Shallots
  (page 83)
Plum sauce, for dipping

1 In a small bowl, stir 1 tablespoon plum sauce orange juice and soy sauce together. Set aside.
2 Heat the oil in a wok over medium heat and stir-fry the garlic and chili until fragrant, about 1 minute. Add the bok choy and stir-fry for 2 minutes. Add the pork and plum sauce mixture. Stir-fry until the pork changes color, 1–2 minutes. Remove from the heat and let stand for 5 minutes.
3 Place the bread on a clean work surface. Distribute the pork stir-fry evenly over the bread. Top with the fried noodles and shallots. Roll into a cylinder and wrap in a strip of parchment paper. Cut each roll in half crosswise. Serve immediately, with the plum sauce.

Makes 24 rolls

Thai Beef Salad Wraps

It's hard to resist the spicy, tangy, and sweet and sour flavors of Thai Beef Salad, known as *Yam Neua*. Served here as an informal wrap, your guests will enjoy this popular salad as an easy-to-eat party snack or appetizer. You can substitute the beef with the same amount of shrimp or firm tofu, though for best results, marinate tofu for 6 to 8 hours.

8 fresh chives
Handful of dried cellophane noodles
8 oz (250 g) tender beef steak
1 tablespoon soy sauce
2 cloves garlic, crushed
1 tablespoon rice wine, sake or dry sherry
4 butter lettuce leaves
$1/2$ English (hothouse) cucumber, deseeded and thinly sliced
1 bird's-eye chili, deseeded and sliced
2 tablespoons chopped coriander leaves (cilantro)
2 tablespoons fresh mint leaves
$1/2$ cup (25 g) fresh bean spouts
$1/4$ cup (45 g) unsalted roasted peanuts
4 flour tortillas

Dressing
1 tablespoon lime juice
1 tablespoon fish sauce
1 clove garlic, crushed
2 teaspoons shaved palm sugar or dark brown sugar

1 Put the chives in a small bowl and add enough boiling water to cover. Let stand for 30 seconds or until softened. Drain and rinse under cold water. Set aside.

2 Put the noodles in a bowl and add enough boiling water to cover. Let soak for 10 minutes. Drain. Using scissors, coarsely cut the noodles into short lengths.

3 Put the rump steak in a shallow dish. In a small bowl, stir the soy sauce, garlic and wine together. Pour over the steak, cover and refrigerate for 30 minutes. Drain. Pat steak dry with paper towels.

4 Heat a grill pan over medium–high heat. Brush the pan with oil, add the steak and cook for 2 minutes on each side for rare. Remove from the pan and let cool. Slice thinly across the grain. Set aside.

5 Remove bottom 2 inches (5 cm) of stem from the lettuce leaves. In a bowl, combine the steak, noodles, cucumber, chili, coriander leaves, mint, bean sprouts and peanuts.

6 In a small bowl, stir all the Dressing ingredients together until the sugar dissolves. Add to the salad and toss to coat evenly.

7 Warm the flour tortillas according to instructions on the packet. Place the tortillas on a clean work surface. Place a lettuce leaf on one side of each tortilla. Spoon the salad over. Roll up and tie with 1 chive at each end of the roll. Cut the rolls in half crosswise to serve.

Makes 4 rolls

Seafood Wraps with Sweet Sour Sauce

These festive yet simple-to-make seafood wraps follow in the tradition of the sensational taste and texture of two-in-one wrapped hors d'oeurves—think pigs in a blanket or bacon-wrapped scallops. In this recipe the shrimp is wrapped with a piece of fish, then lightly seasoned, breaded and fried.

8 boneless, skinless white fish fillets (about 5 oz/150 g each), cut in half horizontally
16 jumbo shrimp (king prawns), shelled and deveined (tails intact)
1 tablespoon oil
1 tablespoon fresh lime juice
2 cloves garlic, finely chopped
1 egg, beaten with 3 tablespoons milk
$^1/_2$ cup (15 g) dried bread crumbs
Oil for deep-frying
Bottled sweet and sour sauce or Thai sweet chili sauce, for dipping

1 Wrap 1 piece of fish around each shrimp and secure with a toothpick. In a small bowl, stir 1 tablespoon of oil with the lime juice and garlic. Brush the wrapped rolls with the oil mixture, then cover with plastic wrap and refrigerate for 30 minutes.
2 Dip the wrapped rolls in the egg mixture, then dredge in the bread crumbs. In a large wok or deep fryer, heat the oil to 375°F (190°C) or until a small bread cube dropped in the oil sizzles and turns golden. Working in batches, fry the seafood wraps until golden, 2–3 minutes. Using a slotted spoon, transfer to paper towels to drain. Serve hot, with the chili sauce for dipping.

Makes 16 wraps

Classic Fried Wontons with Hoisin Dip

In this classic recipe, duck, orange and hoisin sauce create a wonderfully rich flavor.

1 cup (185 g) shredded Chinese roast duck, chicken or turkey meat with skin
2 green onions (scallions), finely chopped
1 teaspoon grated fresh ginger
1 teaspoon grated orange rind
2 tablespoons hoisin sauce
$1/2$ teaspoon sesame oil
16–20 square wonton wrappers
Oil for deep-frying

Dipping sauce
2 tablespoons hoisin sauce
1 tablespoon Chinese black vinegar
1 teaspoon sesame oil

1 In a bowl, combine the meat, green onions, ginger and orange rind. Stir in the hoisin sauce and sesame oil until well combined.
2 Place 1 wonton wrapper on a clean work surface (keep remaining skins covered with a damp cloth to prevent drying out). Place 2 teaspoonfuls of the meat mixture in the center. Brush the edges of the wrapper with water. Gather the edges together and twist to seal. Repeat with remaining wonton wrappers and filling.
3 In a wok or deep fryer, heat the oil until smoking. Fry the wontons in batches until golden, 1–2 minutes. Using a slotted spoon, transfer to paper towels to drain.
4 In a small bowl, mix all the Dipping Sauce ingredients together. Serve the wontons hot, with the Dipping Sauce.

Makes 16–20 wontons

Siew Mai Dumplings with Chili Oil

These mouthwatering open-faced dumplings are a Southeast Asian twist on a Chinese dumpling that is popular dim sum fare. Traditionally dim sum consists of a variety of small snacks served in Chinese teahouses throughout the day. I enjoy serving Siew Mai Dumplings at parties and as appetizers.

5 oz (150 g) ground pork
5 oz (150 g) jumbo shrimp (king prawns), shelled and deveined
2 cloves garlic, finely chopped
1 tablespoon grated fresh ginger
$1/4$ teaspoon salt
2 tablespoons chopped coriander leaves (cilantro)
1 tablespoon chopped Vietnamese mint (laksa leaf) or Thai basil
16 wonton wrappers

Chili Oil
1 tablespoon chili oil
2 teaspoons sweet black soy sauce or hoisin sauce
1 tablespoon finely chopped garlic
1 teaspoon Chinese red vinegar

Makes 12 dumplings

1 In a food processor, combine the pork, shrimp, garlic, ginger and salt. Process for 20 seconds or until well blended. Transfer to a bowl and add the coriander and mint leaves. Using wet hands, mix until well combined.

2 Place the wonton wrappers on a clean work surface. Cover the remaining wrappers with a clean damp kitchen towel. Place 1 tablespoon of the pork filling onto the center of the wonton wrapper. Brush the edges of the wrapper with water. Gather the edges around the filling, forming a basket. Gently squeeze the center of the dumpling so that the filling is exposed at the top. Tap the base of the dumpling on the work surface to flatten. Set aside on a tray and cover with plastic wrap. Repeat with the remaining wonton wrappers and filling.

3 Place the dumplings in a steamer or steamer basket lined with parchment (baking) paper, leaving some space for steam to circulate efficiently. Partially fill a wok or pot with water (steamer or basket should not touch the water) and bring to a rapid boil. Place the steamer over the boiling water and cover. Steam for 12 minutes, adding more water to the wok if necessary.

4 Meanwhile, stir all the Chili Oil ingredients together in a small bowl.

5 Lift the steamer or steamer basket off the wok and carefully remove the dumplings from the steamer. Serve hot, with the Chili Oil for dipping.

Sushi Rice

The first step in making sushi is to prepare the rice. It is well worth buying an electric rice cooker, as it reduces the process of cooking the rice to the simple press of a button. After cooking the rice, you will need a wooden sushi bowl and rice paddle or a large non-metallic mixing or salad bowl and a wooden spatula to make the sushi rice. Do not use metallic utensils as the vinegar used to make sushi rice can react with metal and cause an unpleasant taste.

$1\frac{1}{2}$ cups (300 g) uncooked short-grain
  Japanese rice
$1\frac{1}{2}$ cups (375 ml) water
1 tablespoon mirin or sake

Vinegar Dressing
4 tablespoons rice vinegar
2 tablespoons sugar
1 teaspoon salt

Makes 4 cups (600 g) Sushi Rice
Preparation time: 15 mins + 30 mins soaking
Cooking time: 25 mins

1 Using a measuring cup, measure the required amount of rice and place it into a bowl that holds at least twice the volume of the rice.
2 Wash the rice by adding water to the bowl. Stir the rice briskly for about 10 seconds, then cover it with your hand and carefully drain away the milky water. Repeat this process until the water runs clear. Transfer the rice to a sieve to drain. Set aside for 30 minutes.
3 Place all the ingredients and the washed rice in the electric rice cooker and allow the rice to soak for 20 to 30 minutes—the rice grains will absorb moisture and start to swell. Then switch on the rice cooker.

Note: If not using an electric rice cooker, place all the ingredients in a heavy saucepan. Soak the rice for 20–30 minutes, then bring to a boil over medium heat. Boil the rice for 1–2 minutes, then cover the pan tightly, reduce the heat to low and simmer for 10–20 minutes until cooked. Turn off the heat and allow the cooked rice to steam for 20 minutes before removing the lid.

Do not refrigerate cooked Sushi Rice, as this causes the gluten to congeal and reduces the stickiness of the rice, making it hard to shape properly, as well as reducing the flavor. Prepared Sushi Rice will not keep until the next day.

4 Prepare the Vinegar Dressing by combining the rice vinegar, sugar and salt in a small saucepan and heat over low heat, stirring occasionally, until the sugar is dissolved. Remove from the heat and set aside to cool. To stop the vinegar from distilling off, set the bowl of vinegar in a cold water bath to speed up the cooling process.

5 Wipe the inside of a wooden bowl with a damp cloth to moisten it slightly and moisten the rice paddle with water. Transfer the cooked rice to the wooden bowl while it is still hot using the rice paddle.

6 Slowly pour the Vinegar Dressing evenly over the cooked rice, a little at a time and mix it into the rice with quick cutting strokes (not stirring) of the paddle across the bowl to separate the rice grains and spread the rice out. At the same time, fan the rice to cool it quickly by using a hand-held fan or an electric fan set at low. This will give a glossy finish to the rice. Continue until the rice is lukewarm. It should take about 10 minutes to mix in the sushi rice vinegar sauce thoroughly.

7 Spread a damp muslin cloth or kitchen towel over the rice to keep it moist and cover the bowl until ready to use.

Nigiri Sushi

The most popular type of sushi served in restaurants, this simple-to-make sushi is sure to impress your guests.

2 cups (300 g) cooked Sushi Rice (page 62)
7 oz (200 g) raw fish (salmon or tuna), sliced into 16 strips measuring $2^1/_2$ x $1^1/_4$ x $^1/_4$ in (6 x 3 x $^1/_2$ cm) or other toppings of your choice
Wasabi paste, to taste
Japanese Pickled Ginger (purchased), to serve
Soy sauce, for dipping

Tezu Vinegar Water
1 cup (250 ml) water
2 tablespoons rice vinegar
1 teaspoon salt

Note: Buy only sushi-grade fish. Before using salmon, cover it with salt and marinate for 1 hour, then rinse off the salt and place it in the freezer.

Makes 16 sushi

1 Prepare the Sushi Rice by following the recipe on page 62.
2 Put the Tezu Vinegar Water ingredients in a bowl and mix well.
3 To shape the rice, first moisten your hands in the bowl of Tezu to prevent the rice from sticking to your hands, then take 2 tablespoons of the Sushi Rice and shape it into an oval "finger", pressing it gently to form a small log. Pick up a slice of the topping using your left hand and dab a little wasabi (if using) on it with your right index finger.
4 Place the rice "finger" on top of the topping and press it onto the wasabi-dabbed topping with your index finger. Then turn the rice and topping over so that the topping is on top. Using your index finger and middle finger, mold the topping around the rice, pressing it gently around the rice so that the rice does not show around the edges of the topping. Repeat with the remaining ingredients to make a total of 16 sushi.
5 Arrange the sushi on a serving platter and serve immediately with mounds of wasabi paste, Japanese Pickled Ginger and small dipping bowls of soy sauce.

Step-by-step Nigiri Sushi

1 Hold a slice of the topping with your left hand. Using the tip of your right index finger, dab a little wasabi on the topping.

2 Using your index finger, press the rice onto the wasabi-dabbed topping.

3 Turn over so that topping is on top. Use your index and middle fingers to mold and gently press topping down onto the rice.

Thin Nori Sushi Rolls with Tuna or Salmon

These thin rolls are a classic part of a traditional sushi meal. Simple yet elegant, they are easy to assemble once your ingredients are prepped and in place. And sashimi-grade fish is increasingly available in the West in Asian markets and in non-Asian fish markets.

4 cups cooked Sushi Rice (page 62)
4 oz (125 g) fresh sashimi-grade tuna or
    salmon fillet, pin bones and skin removed
2 sheets toasted nori seaweed sheets
About $1/4$–$1/2$ teaspoon wasabi paste
Soy sauce, for dipping

Tezu Vinegar Water
1 cup (250 ml) water
2 tablespoons rice vinegar
1 teaspoon salt

Makes about 24 pieces

1 Prepare the Sushi Rice by following the recipe on page 62.
2 Put the Tezu Vinegar Water ingredients in a bowl and mix well.
3 Cut the salmon into $3/8$-inch (1-cm) square sticks. Place a sushi mat on a clean work surface. Cut each nori sheet in half. Place 1 piece nori on the sushi mat.
4 First moisten your hands in the bowl of Tezu to prevent the rice from sticking to your hands, put 2–3 tablespoonfuls of the prepared Sushi Rice in one hand. Make a log shape with the Rice and place it in the center of the nori. Using your hands, spread the Rice evenly over the nori, leaving a $1/2$-inch (12-mm) border. Take a small dot of wasabi paste and draw a line down the center of the Rice.
5 Arrange a stick of salmon over the wasabi. Pick up the sushi mat from the side nearest to you. Roll the mat over to meet the other side, making sure the Rice stays inside the nori. Lift the top edge of the mat and press and roll the cylinder slightly, seam-side down. Transfer to a cutting board. Repeat with the remaining nori, Sushi Rice and filling.
6 To serve, cut each roll into 6 pieces. Serve with soy sauce for dipping.

Inside-out California Rolls

Though these thick-style inside-out sushi rolls originated in the Osaka area of Japan, many variations have sprung up around the world—including the California roll, the most famous variation in the West. This festive variation is studded with both black and white sesame seeds.

3 cups (450 g) cooked Sushi rice (page 62)
2 sheets nori seaweed
1 tablespoon combined toasted black and white sesame seeds
1–2 tablespoons wasabi paste or to taste
Soy sauce, for dipping

Tezu Vinegar Water
1 cup (250 ml) water
2 tablespoons rice vinegar
1 teaspoon salt

Fillings
1 avocado, pitted and peeled, then cut into strips
4 tablespoons flying fish roe
2 tablespoons wasabi paste
$1/2$ English (hothouse) cucumber, deseeded and thinly sliced
4 sticks crab sticks

Note: Crab sticks are made of surimi, or finely pulverized white fish flesh, that has been shaped and cured to resemble snow crab legs. They are usually red and white in color, and rectangular in shape. The smell is similar to any seafood product and the taste is slightly salty. Crab sticks are cooked during the curing process and can be eaten directly from the package. They are sold in plastic packets in most supermarkets.

1 Prepare the Sushi Rice by following the recipe on page 62.
2 Put the Tezu Vinegar Water ingredients in a bowl and mix well.
3 Cut each piece of nori in half lengthwise. Place one half nori sheet along the long side of a bamboo mat nearest to you. To shape the rice, first moisten your hands in the bowl of Tezu Vinegar Water to prevent the rice from sticking to your hands. Spread one quarter of the Rice evenly over the nori. Gently rake your fingers across the grains to spread the Rice. Sprinkle the Rice with the mixed sesame seeds and cover with a large sheet of plastic wrap.
4 Pick up the mat, carefully turn over so the nori is now on top and place back on the mat. Spread a pinch of wasabi and selection of Fillings across the center of the nori. Make sure the Fillings extend completely to each end. Using your index finger and thumb, pick up the edge of the bamboo mat and plastic wrap nearest to you. Place your other fingers over the Fillings to hold them as you roll the mat forward tightly, wrapping the Rice and nori around the Fillings. Press gently and continue rolling forward to complete the roll. Gently press the mat to shape and seal the roll. Unroll the mat and plastic.
5 Wipe a sharp knife with a damp cloth and cut the roll to make 8 pieces, wiping the knife after each cut. Serve with the remaining wasabi and soy sauce.

Makes 4 rolls (32 pieces)

Smoked Salmon and Cream Cheese Sushi

This pretty inside-out roll with smoked salmon is a wonderfully inventive western twist on sushi.

1 nori seaweed sheet
1 cup (150 g) cooked Sushi Rice (page 62)
1 teaspoon wasabi paste or English mustard
2 tablespoons cream cheese
4 slices smoked salmon
4 asparagus spears, blanched and chilled
4 fresh dill sprigs, minced
Soy sauce, for dipping

Makes 8 pieces

1 Cover a sushi mat with plastic wrap. Place nori on the plastic, glossy side down. Spread the Sushi Rice over the nori, leaving a $3/4$-inch (2-cm) uncovered strip of nori on side farthest from you. Holding the surface of the Rice with one hand, turn over the rice and nori so that the rice is on the plastic and nori is on top. Using your index finger, smear the wasabi and cream cheese over the nori.
2 Arrange 2 salmon slices and 2 asparagus spears in the center, allowing the asparagus to poke out of the nori at both ends. Roll the sushi to enclose the fillings but leave one-fourth of the nori visible at the end farthest from you. Lift up the mat and roll forward to join the nori edges. Press gently to form into a square shape.
3 Unroll the mat, remove the plastic and transfer roll to a cutting board. Wipe a sharp knife, cut the roll into 4 pieces. Coat the rolls with dill. Place the rolls on plates and serve with soy sauce.

Shrimp Sushi Rolls

Dressed in black, these elegant rolls are ready for a dinner party or a night of entertaining.

1 nori seaweed sheet, halved
2 cups (300 g) cooked Sushi Rice (page 62)
4 deep-fried battered jumbo shrimp or barbecued shrimp
4 fresh Thai basil or shiso leaves
1 hard-boiled egg yolk, crumbled

Thai Basil Sauce
1 tablespoon rice vinegar
1 teaspoon fish sauce
Leaves from 2 Thai basil sprigs, chopped
1 teaspoon packed brown sugar

Makes 8 pieces

1 Make the Thai Basil Sauce by combining all the ingredients in a bowl and mix well. Set aside.
2 Arrange one half sheet of nori, glossy side down, on a sushi mat. With wet fingers, spread half the Sushi Rice evenly over the nori, leaving uncovered a $3/4$-inch (2-cm) strip of nori on side farthest from you. Place 2 shrimp over the Rice, allowing the tails to poke out at both ends of the nori. Top with 2 basil leaves and roll. If nori is too dry to seal, wet the edge and press with the mat.
3 Unroll the mat and transfer the roll to a cutting board. Wipe a sharp knife with a damp towel and cut each roll into 4 pieces, wiping knife after each cut. Repeat with the remaining ingredients. Arrange the pieces on serving plates and sprinkle the sieved egg yolk over the shrimp tails. Serve with the Thai Basil Sauce.

New York Sirloin Sushi Rolls

These unique square-shaped rolls are as eye-catching as they are delicious. Filled with tender, rare steak and served with a Thai Basil Sauce, these sushi rolls are sure to win your meat-loving guests over with one bite.

Oil, for deep-frying
1 green onion (scallion), thinly sliced lengthwise into long shreds
1 carrot, peeled and finely shredded
1 tablespoon oil
1 sirloin steak (about $1/4$ lb/125 g)
$3/4$ nori sheet
1 cup (150 g) cooked Sushi Rice (page 62)
2 fresh coriander leaves (cilantro)
1 clove garlic, crushed
$1/4$ teaspoon wasabi paste or English mustard

Thai Basil Sauce
1 tablespoon rice vinegar
1 teaspoon fish sauce
2 fresh Thai basil leaves, finely chopped
1 teaspoon brown sugar

1 Prepare the Sushi Rice by following the recipe on page 62.
2 Fill a tempura pan or deep-fryer one-third full with oil and heat over medium-high heat to 365°F (185°C). Fry the green onion until golden brown. Using a slotted spoon, transfer to paper towels to drain. Repeat with the carrot. Set aside.
3 Combine all the Thai Basil Sauce ingredients in a bowl and mix well. Set aside.
4 Heat 1 tablespoon oil in a frying pan over medium heat and cook the sirloin, turning once, about 10 seconds on each side. Transfer to a plate to cool, and once it has cooled, slice thinly across the grain.
5 Place the nori on a bamboo mat, glossy side down and spread the Sushi Rice over it. Place the sirloin slices over three-quarters of the nori, toward the front and with wet hands spread the Sushi Rice over the sirloin. With your index finger, smear the wasabi and garlic across the center. Top with the coriander leaves.
6 Using your index finger and thumb, pick up the edge of the mat nearest to you. Place your remaining fingers over the fillings to hold them as you roll the mat forward tightly. Press gently and continue rolling forward to complete the roll. Gently press the mat to shape and seal the roll. Unroll the mat and transfer the roll to a cutting board.
7 With a dampened knife, slice the roll in half. Place 2 pieces side by side and cut them in half; then cut each half again to make a total of 8 pieces, wiping the knife after each cut.
8 Top 4 pieces with fried onion and the remaining 4 pieces with carrot. Serve with the Thai basil sauce.

Makes 8 pieces

Tofu and Sweet Sesame Sushi Wraps

Known as inari sushi in Japan, these golden tofu pouches are filled with a mixture of sushi rice and other ingredients.

$4^1/_2$ cups (675 g) cooked Sushi Rice (page 62)

6 green onions (scallions), white part only, finely sliced (reserve green parts for tying)

$1^1/_2$ tablespoons black sesame seeds

12 fried tofu pouches (abura-age)

Soy sauce, for dipping

Makes 12

1 Prepare the Sushi Rice by following the recipe on page 62.

2 Cut the green onion greens in half lengthwise. Put in a bowl and add enough boiling water to cover. Let stand for 15 seconds. Drain and rinse in cold running water. Put aside.

3 In a bowl, combine the Sushi Rice, sesame seeds and sliced green onions. Mix well. In a saucepan of boiling water, boil the tofu skins for 3 minutes. Using a slotted spoon, transfer to paper towels to drain. Let cool.

4 Cut each tofu skin in half. Open each half to make a pouch. Using wet hands, scoop up about $1/_4$ cup (35 g) rice mixture and put into a tofu pouch; do not overfill or the pouch will split. Put the filled pouches, open-side up, on a plate. Tie a green onion length around each tofu pouch. Refrigerate for $1/_2$ hour before serving. Serve with the soy sauce for dipping.

1 In a saucepan of boiling water, blanch the tofu skins for 3 minutes. Using a slotted spoon, transfer to paper towels to drain. Cut each tofu skin in half. Open each half to make a pouch.

2 Using wet hands, place about $1/_4$ cup of the sushi rice mixture into a tofu pouch. Do not overfill or the pouch will split. Put the filled pouches, open-side up, on a cutting board or plate.

3 Tie a green onion length around each tofu pouch. Refrigerate for $1/_2$ hour before serving.

Salmon or Tuna Sashimi

With no rice, sesame seeds or other adornments, sashimi is for the unabashed lovers of raw fish. Sashimi is traditionally served with a condiment such as shredded daikon radish or fresh ginger and a simple dipping sauce. If you prefer cooked fish to raw, lightly sear or poach the fish for a few seconds on each side so it is cooked outside but still rare inside, then slice.

$1/_2$ cup (125 g) grated or shredded root vegetable such as daikon radish, carrot or beet, as garnish
10 oz (300 g) sashimi-grade salmon or tuna fillet without skin, bones removed
Wasabi paste, for serving
Soy sauce, for dipping

Serves 4

1 Hold the fish fillet in your left hand, place the sharp edge of the knife perpendicular to the fillet and cut into slices $1/_2$ inch (12 mm) wide. While cutting each slice, slide the knife from base to tip of blade in one continuous movement, then move remaining whole fillet, away from cut slices, using the tip of the knife. Do not push the cut pieces away.
2 Place the grated or shredded vegetable on the serving plate and arrange the salmon or tuna slices on top of the shredded vegetable.
3 Serve with wasabi and soy sauce in small dipping bowls.

Simple Nori Tuna Rolls

Nearly unadorned as the sashimi shown opposite, these streamlined rolls consist merely of tuna rolled in a sheet of nori. Served with simple condiments of soy sauce for dipping and wasabi, these easy-to-assemble rolls make an elegant appetizer.

10 oz (300g) sashimi-grade tuna
4 nori seaweed sheets, halved
$^1/_2$ cup (125 g) shredded daikon radish or beet
Wasabi paste, for serving
Soy sauce, for dipping

Serves 4

1 Cut the tuna into cylinders 1 inch (2.5 cm) in diameter and 4 inches (10 cm) long.
2 Lay a halved nori sheet on a clean, dry board and top with 1 tuna slice. Roll up tightly using both hands. Repeat with the remaining tuna slices and nori sheets. Cut each roll into 4 pieces. Divide the daikon between 4 bowls. Place 4 rolls in each bowl. Garnish with the beet flower and cucumber leaves. Serve with wasabi and soy sauce for dipping.

Note: When slicing rolled tuna on a board, keep the board dry or the nori will become soggy. Salmon may be substituted for tuna.

Grilled Tofu Cubes

Dengaku is one of Japan's favorite and simplest ways of serving tofu. Firm, bite-sized pieces or slices of tofu are delicious and nutritious snacks when lightly grilled until golden, spread with miso or other toppings and lightly grilled again until fragrant. Marinating the tofu before grilling adds extra flavor. Teriyaki sauce, barbecue sauce, plum sauce, sweet black soy sauce or sweet and sour sauce, may all be used as marinades, but you may need to adjust the grilling time to keep the sugar in the marinade from burning.

1 lb (500 g) firm tofu, drained and pressed
$1/4$ cup (60 ml) soy sauce
2 tablespoons water
3 tablespoons mirin or sweet sherry
$1/2$ teaspoon sesame oil
Lime for serving

Serves 4

1 Cut the tofu into bite-sized cubes and place in a flat dish or broiler (grill) pan.
2 Combine the soy sauce, water, mirin and sesame oil and pour over the tofu. Marinate for 15 minutes, turning occasionally. Drain and pat dry with paper towels.
3 Place the tofu on a lightly greased broiler (grill) pan and cook until lightly browned, 3–4 minutes on each side. Skewer a piece of tofu and a piece of lime onto toothpicks and serve.

Deep-fried Tofu Cubes

Agedashi tofu is a classic Japanese tofu dish. Bite-sized blocks of tofu, deep-fried until lightly crisp, are served with a seasoned dashi broth and simple condiments of ginger, green onion and bonito flakes.

1 lb (500 g) firm tofu, drained and pressed
2 tablespoons cornstarch
Oil, for deep-frying
$3/4$ cup (180 ml) dashi stock (page 69)
$2^1/_2$ tablespoons soy sauce
$2^1/_2$ tablespoons mirin or sweet sherry
$1/_4$ cup (60 g) shredded daikon radish
1 tablespoon grated fresh ginger
1 green onion (scallion), green part only
1 tablespoon bonito flakes

Serves 4

1 Cut the tofu into 12 equal cubes. Toss in the cornstarch, shaking off any excess.
2 Fill a frying pan or wok one-third full with oil and heat to 365°F (185°C). Deep-fry the tofu in batches until lightly browned all over, 5–6 minutes. Drain on paper towels.
3 In a small saucepan, combine the stock, soy sauce and mirin and bring to a simmer. Place 3 pieces of tofu in each serving bowl. Arrange the daikon, ginger and onion on top and pour the sauce around the tofu. Sprinkle with bonito flakes and serve immediately.

Note: For a spicy variation, season the cornstarch with chili pepper flakes, fresh herbs or black and white sesame seeds.

Cajun Sushi Rolls

With a dusting of Cajun seasoning mix, these little rolls pack a lot of punch. Though the cooling cream cheese keeps the spice in check, you can add more or less seasoning to match your personal heat index. You can easily find pre-made Cajun seasoning, or you can make your own.

4 smoked salmon slices
1 tablespoon cream cheese
$1/_4$ teaspoon Cajun seasoning mix
1 cup (150 g) cooked Sushi Rice (page 62)
6 green beans, blanched
1 teaspoon shiso (Japanese basil) powder

Makes 8 pieces

1 Cover a sushi mat with plastic wrap. Lay the salmon slices horizontally across the plastic wrap from the edge closest to you.
2 Spread the cream cheese across the center and sprinkle with the Cajun seasoning mix. With wet fingers, spread the Sushi Rice over the salmon slices, leaving $3/_4$ inch (2 cm) uncovered. Place the green beans in a straight line. Roll up very tightly. Repeat with the remaining ingredients.
3 Unroll the mat and transfer the roll to a cutting board. Wipe a sharp knife with a damp towel, cut each roll into 4 pieces, wiping the knife after each cut. Remove the plastic from the rolls.
4 Holding 1 piece, dip the seam side into the shiso powder. Arrange on serving plates.

Crispy Fish Fingers

Breaded and fried fish sticks or "nuggets" have become so ubiquitous in our fast-food culture that it's easy to forget that, when done right, breaded and fried fresh fish is delicious. In this recipe, the fish is marinated in a zesty seasoning paste, giving these fingers a very exotic taste.

$1/2$ onion, grated
3 cloves garlic, finely chopped
2 teaspoons ground coriander seeds
$1/2$ teaspoon ground red pepper (cayenne)
1 teaspoon ground black pepper
1 tablespoon fresh lemon juice
1 teaspoon salt
1 tablespoon oil
4 white fish fillets (6 oz/180 g each)
1 cup (150 g) all-purpose (plain) flour

Serves 4

1 In a food processor, combine the onion, garlic, ground coriander, ground red pepper, black pepper, lemon juice, salt and oil. Process to a paste.
2 Cut the fish fillets into strips. Place them in a baking dish and spread the onion paste over the fish. Cover and refrigerate for 1 hour.
3 Place the flour in a shallow bowl. Coat the fish in the flour, shaking off excess. In a large wok, heat enough oil to 375°F (190°C) or until a small bread cube dropped in the oil sizzles and turns golden in 1 minute. Fry the fish fingers in batches until golden, 1–2 minutes. Using a slotted spoon, transfer to paper towels to drain. Serve immediately, with lime and tomato wedges.

Barbecued Chicken Salad Rolls

This fun twist on Fresh Thai Spring Rolls (page 42) makes a delightful appetizer or a wholesome snack between meals. The filling is marinated in distinctive citrus-based sauce with an exotic touch of pleasantly sour tamarind paste, which is made from the fruit of a tree native to Asia and northern Africa.

Handful of dried cellophane noodles
1 tablespoon dried shrimp, finely chopped
  or ground in a mortar and pestle
8 cherry tomatoes, quartered
$1/2$ red onion, thinly sliced
1–2 red bird's-eye chilies, deseeded and
  chopped to taste
2 tablespoons chopped fresh basil
2 tablespoons roasted peanuts
8 oz (250 g) roasted chicken meat, deboned
8 round rice paper wrappers (8 inches /20
  cm in diameter)
4 butter lettuce leaves
1 tablespoon Crispy Fried Shallots
  (see note)
Ginger Lime Dip (page 16)

Dressing
1 tablespoon fresh lime juice
1 tablespoon fish sauce
1 teaspoon tamarind pulp
2 teaspoons granulated sugar

Makes 4 rolls

1 Put the noodles in a bowl and add enough boiling water to cover. Let soak for 10 minutes. Drain. Using scissors, coarsely cut the noodles into shorter lengths. In a bowl, combine the shrimp, tomatoes, onion, chili, basil, peanuts and noodles. Stir until well combined.
2 Cut the chicken meat and skin into thin strips about $2^1/_2$ inches (6 cm) long. Combine all the Dressing ingredients in a screwtop jar and shake to mix. Add the chicken and Dressing to the noodle mixture. Toss to combine. Cover and refrigerate for at least 30 minutes or up to 1 hour.
3 Remove about 2 inches (5 cm) of center stem from each lettuce leaf. Fill a medium bowl with warm water and place a kitchen towel on your work surface. Stack the wrappers on a damp kitchen towel to prevent from drying out. For each roll, dip 2 rice paper wrappers into the water for 15 seconds or until soft.
4 Divide the chicken mixture into 4 portions. Arrange a lettuce leaf on one side of the rice paper. Spoon over 1 portion of the chicken mixture. Sprinkle with the fried shallots and spread the mixture over the lettuce leaf. Starting at lettuce side of wrapper, roll into a cylinder. Cover the prepared rolls with a damp kitchen towel to prevent from drying out. Repeat with the remaining wrappers and filling.
5 Using a sharp knife, cut each roll into 2 or 3 slices. Serve with the Ginger Lime dip (page 16).

Note: Make the **Crispy Fried Shallots** by heating 1 cup (250 ml) oil in a small saucepan over medium heat and fry 10–15 thinly sliced shallots until golden brown and crisp, 2–3 minutes. Be careful not to burn. Fried Shallots can be made ahead and stored in an airtight container. They are also available at Asian markets.

Curried Shrimp Rolls

Indian cuisine is appreciated for its rich complexity of flavors worldwide, and these Curried Shrimp Rolls are no exception. The list of ingredients for this appetizer is a bit longer than some in this book, but the extra time it takes to assemble and prepare them is well worth the mouth-watering result.

1 tablespoon oil
2 teaspoons sesame oil
1 teaspoon cumin seeds
1 clove garlic, finely chopped
1 tablespoon grated fresh ginger
1 finger-length green chili pepper, deseeded and finely chopped
1 teaspoon ground turmeric
1 teaspoon ground red pepper (cayenne)
1 lb (500 g) potatoes, peeled, boiled and diced
$1/2$ cup (75 g) fresh or frozen peas
$1/2$ teaspoon salt
1 tablespoon chopped coriander leaves (cilantro)
1 tablespoon chopped mint leaves
12 frozen spring roll wrappers, about 8 inches (20 cm), thawed
1 egg white, lightly beaten
Oil for deep-frying
Thai sweet chili sauce and soy sauce, for dipping

1 In a wok or large skillet, heat the oils over medium heat. Add the cumin seeds, garlic, ginger, green chili peppers, turmeric and ground red pepper. Fry for 1 minute. Stir in the potatoes, peas and salt and fry for 1 minute. Remove from the heat and let cool completely. Stir in the coriander and mint leaves.
2 Place 1 spring roll wrapper on a clean work surface. Place 1 heaped tablespoon of the filling in the center of the wrapper. Fold over the sides and then roll up diagonally. Seal the loose edge with the egg white. Repeat with the remaining wrappers and filling.
3 In a wok or deep fryer, heat the oil to 375°F (190°C) or until a small bread cube dropped in the oil sizzles and turns golden in 1 minute. Add the spring rolls in batches and fry until golden, about 2 minutes. Using a slotted spoon, transfer to paper towels to drain. Serve immediately with the Thai sweet chili sauce and soy sauce.

Makes 12 rolls

Stuffed Tofu Triangles

Tofu and pork are a classic Asian combination, and in this recipe a savory pork filling is sandwiched between pillowy soft tofu cushions that have been fried to form a crusty golden-brown exterior. To make this appetizer vegetarian, replace the pork with minced tempeh or black Chinese mushrooms.

8 oz (250 g) ground pork or chicken
2 tablespoons finely sliced green onions (scallions)
1 tablespoon sake
$1/4$ teaspoon sesame oil
2 teaspoons cornstarch
1 tablespoon soy sauce
$1/2$ teaspoon grated fresh ginger
2 cakes firm tofu (10 oz/300 g each), drained and pressed
Cornstarch for coating
Oil, for deep-frying
Mixed salad greens, for serving
Soy sauce, for dipping

1 In a medium bowl, combine the pork or chicken, green onion, sake, sesame oil, potato flour, soy sauce and ginger. Mix well.
2 Cut the tofu in half, then cut each half diagonally to make 4 triangles. Scoop out a small spoonful of tofu on the long diagonal side of each triangle and stuff the opening with the meat mixture, being careful not to break the tofu. Dredge each triangle in the cornstarch.
3 Fill a frying pan or wok with oil one-third full and heat to 365°F (185°C) and deep-fry the tofu triangles, until golden and the meat is cooked, 2–3 minutes on each side. Turn the tofu carefully so it doesn't break. Drain on paper towels and serve immediately with the salad greens and extra soy sauce.

Note: For a spicy version, flavor the cornstarch for coating the tofu triangles with curry powder or chili pepper flakes. For a breaded version, omit the cornstarch coating and dip the tofu into lightly beaten egg, then dredge in coarse breadcrumbs.

Makes 8 triangles

Crisp Tuna and Basil Spring Rolls

These pretty pink and green spring rolls can be served whole or, in a quasi-sushi style, sliced into rounds. To enjoy the tuna rare to medium-rare, which is what we recommend, cook the rolls as directed. If you prefer the tuna medium to well-done, cook it for an additional 1–2 minutes.

8-oz (500-g) piece sashimi-quality tuna
1–2 teaspoons wasabi paste, or to taste
8 large basil or shiso leaves
8 frozen square (8 by 8 inches/20 by 20 cm) spring roll wrappers, thawed
1 egg white, lightly beaten
Oil for deep-frying
Soy sauce, for dipping

Makes 8 rolls

1 Using a sharp knife, cut the tuna into slices ³/₄ inch (2 cm) wide and 3 inches (7.5 cm) long. Lightly spread each piece of tuna with wasabi paste.
2 Wrap each piece of tuna in a basil or shiso leaf (trim leaf to size if necessary). Place a spring roll wrapper on a clean work surface with one end facing you. Brush the wrapper with egg white. Place a tuna parcel 1 inch (2.5 cm) from the end of the wrapper. Roll the bottom of the wrapper over. Fold in the sides and roll up. Cover with plastic wrap. Repeat with remaining wrappers and filling.
3 In a wok or a deep fryer, heat the oil to 375°F (190°C) or until a small bread cube dropped in the oil sizzles and turns golden. Working in batches, lower the tuna rolls and fry until golden, 1–2 minutes. Using a slotted spoon, transfer to paper towels to drain. Serve immediately, whole or sliced, with soy sauce for dipping.

1 Using a sharp knife, cut the tuna into slices ³/₄ inch (2 cm) wide by 3 inches (7.5 cm) long.

2 Lightly spread each piece of tuna with wasabi paste. Wrap each piece of tuna in a basil or shiso leaf (trim leaf to size if necessary).

3 Place a tuna parcel 1 inch (2.5 cm) from end of wrapper. Roll the bottom of the wrapper over, fold in the sides and roll up.

Pork and Shrimp Noodle Rolls

These refreshing rolls, in the tradition of the summer or salad roll, are very easy to assemble once the shrimp and pork are prepared. Served with an irresistible peanut butter-based Satay Peanut Sauce, these rolls are always popular among my guests.

Handful of dried cellophane noodles
4 butter lettuce leaves, thick stem parts removed
4 tablespoons mayonnaise
8 dried rice paper wrappers (8 inches/ 20 cm) in diameter
12 fresh mint leaves
8 oz (250 g) roast pork or barbecued pork, sliced
4 jumbo shrimp (king prawns), cooked, shelled and deveined, then halved
Satay Peanut Sauce (page 16)

Makes 4 rolls

1 Put the noodles in a bowl and add enough boiling water to cover. Let soak for 10 minutes. Drain. Using scissors, coarsely cut the noodles into shorter lengths.
2 Fill a medium bowl with warm water. Place a kitchen towel on your work surface. For each roll, dip 2 rice paper wrappers into the water for 15 seconds or until soft. Stack the wrappers on the towel.
3 Place a lettuce leaf on one side of the wrapper. Top with 1 table-spoonful mayonnaise. Arrange one-eighth of noodles and pork over the lettuce leaf. Top with 3 mint leaves. Starting at lettuce side of the wrapper, roll halfway into a cylinder. Place 2 shrimp halves, cut-side down, on the wrapper. Continue to roll into a cylinder.
4 Cover the rolls with a damp towel to prevent drying out. Repeat with remaining wrappers and filling. Using a sharp knife, cut each roll in half crosswise. Serve with the Satay Peanut Sauce (page 16).

1 Place a lettuce leaf on one side of the stacked papers. Top with 1 tablespoonful of mayonnaise. Arrange the noodles and pork over the lettuce leaf. Top with 3 mint leaves.

2 Starting at lettuce side of wrapper, roll halfway into a cylinder. Lay 2 shrimp halves, cut-side down, on the wrapper.

3 Fold the edges over and roll up. Cover the rolls with a damp towel until ready to serve.

Shrimp Toast Rolls with Cilantro and Chili

These delicate rolls combine everyday, easy-to-find ingredients to create a delicious, tempting appetizer or elegant party nosh. For variety, try these rolls with scallops instead of shrimp.

Filling

8 oz (250 g) fresh jumbo shrimp, peeled and deveined

2 green onions (scallions), finely chopped

2 cloves garlic, finely chopped

1 bird's-eye red chili, deseeded and chopped

2 tablespoons chopped coriander leaves (cilantro)

12 slices white sandwich bread, crusts trimmed

Oil for deep-frying

Thai sweet chili sauce or bottled sweet and sour sauce, for dipping

1 To make the Filling process the shrimp in a food processor until smooth. Transfer to a bowl. Stir in the green onions, garlic, chili and coriander leaves. Mix until well combined. Using a rolling pin, press the bread slices flat. Spread about 1 tablespoonful of the Filling over each slice of bread. Roll up and secure with 2 toothpicks.

2 In a large wok or a deep fryer, heat the oil until it reaches 375°F (190°C) or until a small bread cube dropped in the oil sizzles and turns golden. Working in batches, add the shrimp toast rolls and fry until golden, 1–2 minutes. Using a slotted spoon, transfer to paper towels to drain. Serve hot, with the chili sauce or sweet and sour sauce.

Makes 12 rolls

1 Remove crusts from the bread slices. Roll the bread flat, using a rolling pin.

2 Spread about 1 tablespoonful of the Filling over each slice of bread.

3 Roll up each slice and secure with 2 toothpicks.

Crunchy Tofu Nuggets

Tofu is the tabula rasa of Asian cooking, and this recipe demonstrates just how delicious it can be when it's seasoned with enticing flavors such as soy sauce, fresh ginger and mirin. Ever-versatile tofu also makes a guest appearance in a silky smooth sweet and spicy dipping sauce.

1 cake (10 oz/300 g) firm tofu,
1 cup (250 ml) water
$1/4$ cup (60 ml) soy sauce
1 teaspoon grated fresh ginger
2 tablespoons mirin or sweet white wine
$1/4$ cup (45 g) all-purpose (plain) flour
2 eggs, lightly beaten with 2 tablespoons
   water
$3/4$ cup (60 g) crushed shredded wheat
   breakfast cereal
Oil, for deep-frying

Creamy Sweet Chili Sauce
$3^1/_2$ oz (100 g) silken tofu, drained
$1/4$ cup (60 ml) sweet chili sauce
1 teaspoon soy sauce
1 teaspoon chopped coriander leaves
   (cilantro)

1 In a medium saucepan, combine the tofu, water, soy sauce, ginger and mirin. Gradually bring to a boil, reduce the heat and simmer for 15 minutes, turning the tofu occasionally. Remove from the heat and let cool for 5 minutes.

2 Cut the tofu into 1-inch (2.5 cm) blocks and lightly dust them with the flour. Dip the tofu blocks into the egg mixture, draining off any excess, then dredge them in the crushed wheat flakes.

3 Make the Creamy Sweet Chili Sauce by processing the soft tofu in a blender until smooth. Add the chili sauce, soy sauce and coriander leaves and mix until well combined.

4 Fill a deep saucepan or wok one-third full with oil and heat to 365°F (185°C). Deep-fry the tofu in batches until golden, 2–3 minutes. Drain on paper towels and serve immediately, with the Creamy Sweet Chili Sauce.

Serves 4

Published by Periplus Editions, Ltd., with editorial
offices at 61 Tai Seng Avenue, #02-12, Singapore
534167.

Hardcover ISBN 13: 978-0-7946-0579-7

Distributed by
USA
Tuttle Publishing
364 Innovation Drive,
North Clarendon, VT 05759-9436.
Tel: (802) 773-8930 Fax: (802) 773-6993
info@tuttlepublishing.com
www.tuttlepublishing.com

Asia Pacific
Berkeley Books Pte Ltd.
61 Tai Seng Avenue
#02-12, Singapore 534167.
Tel: (65) 6280-1330 Fax: (65) 6280-6290
inquiries@periplus.com.sg
www.periplus.com

Printed in Singapore
10 09 08   5 4 3 2 1